To Tom and John
Best Wishes

Confessions

of a Recovering
Car Dealer

An Insider's Look at
What Really Goes on
in the Car-Buying
and Service Business

By Earl Stewart

Everything You Need to Know
to Get the Best Price and Best Service

ISBN 978-0-9857295-1-6

All money from the sales of this book will go to charity.
Visit http://www.earlstewarttoyota.com/ to see the list of charities.

Copyright © 2012 by Earl Stewart

Published by Middle River Press
Oakland Park, Florida
middleriverpress.com
First Printing—Printed in the USA

Confessions
of a Recovering
Car Dealer

*An Insider's Look at
What Really Goes on
in the Car-Buying
and Service Business*

By Earl Stewart

Everything You Need to Know
to Get the Best Price and Best Service

MIDDLE
RIVER
PRESS

Foreword

As Earl Stewart's son, I am in the unique position to have witnessed, firsthand and at close range, the transformation of a small town car dealer to an icon in our industry. After fifteen years in the car business, I have come to know many men and women who have occupied every role in the retail and wholesale auto business: hands-on dealers, absentee owners, GMs, managers of all types, and regional and national executives included. I can truly attest that never has there been an individual who has been so utterly distinguished among people like these in terms of vision, intellect, ambition, and personal drive and focus. It is qualities like these that Earl Stewart has put to use to become the transformative figure that he is.

You probably already know who Earl Stewart is. You have read his interviews in *Automotive News* and *The Wall Street Journal*. You have seen him on CNN, FOX News, and your local news broadcasts. When there is big news related to our industry, the media seek him out to get his unique and outspoken perspective on the matter at hand. Absent major events, he is still sought out for his opinion on issues concerning the car business, like the factory/dealer facility wars and stair-step incentives. Earl Stewart is sought out because he has built his reputation and brand on remaking the car business. He sees the future differently than the rest of us and we want to hear what he has to say.

Deserved or not, the car business has been much maligned in American popular culture. We all know this, but Earl is alone in that he recognized this problem and had the courage to accept responsibility for it. He is the first to say, "We brought this upon ourselves." Earl took a hard look at the characteristics and practices that his and most dealerships had that are inherently anti-consumer and realized that if these could be changed, the whole industry could be bettered. If he could do this, his dealerships would become more successful. If he could lead others to do the same, we all could become more successful. So, Earl embarked on remaking his Toyota dealership in Lake Park, Florida. He stopped all advertising that could be construed as misleading or confusing to the customer — none of the old tricks we are so familiar with. He decreed that all profit must come from clear pricing in sales and service and not from add-on fees. He eliminated his $495 dealer fee and his 15% shop fee because he knew those were just ways to sneak in a little more profit from his customers. He knew that the only way he could be sure that any of this could be accomplished is if he made himself available to his customers, so he came out of hiding. He got rid of his secretary, he stopped screening his phone calls, he made his cell and his home phone numbers available to all of his customers and prospective customers, and famously installed red hot-line telephones throughout his dealership that connect customers to him instantly.

It worked. In a short period of time, Earl's Toyota dealership grew from a minor player to the highest volume car dealership in Palm Beach County. His profits soared along with his customer satisfaction scores. Toyota came in to study what he had done after J.D. Power and Associates presented an analysis that showed that Earl Stewart Toyota's customer satisfaction achievements were literally off the chart.

Earl had remade his car dealership, his marketing, and his image; then he told the world about it. He began a consumer advice column in *The Hometown News*, a blog at www.earlstewartoncars.com, and an hour long radio show on a local radio station, Seaview. He embarked on public speaking tours. Using these outlets, Earl "told it like it is" and ruffled a lot of feathers. He became an instant target for other car dealers to attack and was accused of self-aggrandizing at the expense of his fellow dealers. Earl generated controversy wherever he went, but he continued to gain listeners as more and more people began to pay attention. He was attacked by the political right in 2008 when he aired a Spanish-language ad with English subtitles, and was attacked by the left in 2012 when he tried to erect the world's tallest American flag. He drew the ire of car dealers across the state when he testified before the Florida State Senate in his campaign to abolish the dealer fee. He was openly critical of Toyota before local and national media during the sudden acceleration recall crisis and simultaneously pioneered ways to calm terrified customers during this ordeal. In 2012, Earl Stewart is publishing his first book, *Confessions of a Recovering Car Dealer*, a comprehensive consumer's guide to buying and servicing cars.

During his transformation, Earl Stewart assumed the role of warrior whose battles were fought on many fronts. The mistaken impression was that he was in this for himself, but it has never been properly understood that there was a lot more to it. Earl Stewart was, and is, trying to reimagine an old industry in a better fit for our new century. He sees a car business that is more transparent, responsive, and friendly to the consumer. He sees a profession that is worthy of being considered noble — if it can evolve. Every battle he fights is a result of his willingness to go first, even if it's scary, even if it hurts.

My dad begins every radio show by reading a quote from former Toyota North America president, Jim Press:

"The way you treat the customer when you do not owe them anything, like how you treat somebody who cannot fight back, that is the ultimate test of character."

This quote serves as his guiding principle, and he believes it should serve as the guiding principle for all car dealers. It's not entirely an issue of morality; it's an issue of good business sense. If Earl can accomplish this in his dealership, consumers will notice. When it happens at another dealership, more will notice. Perceptions will change. The industry as a whole will change — and it's really happening. Like dominoes falling, one-by-one dealerships around Earl Stewart Toyota began to adopt his best practices, like dropping the dealer fee. A dealer fee free zone has sprung up around Earl Stewart Toyota. As a result of Earl Stewart's crusades, consumers who buy a new Toyota in Palm Beach County will not pay a dealer fee! Consumers in Palm Beach County are now treated to a more transparent, fairer transaction wherever they buy a Toyota, thanks to my dad.

Leaders are not always popular, especially when they are making you eat your broccoli. It is history that allows us to get a clear picture of where our leaders have taken us and time will tell whether Earl Stewart was brilliantly prescient or just a great idea man whose movement never fully got under way. It is too soon to tell. However, it is not in his DNA to do anything halfway and he intends to see the mission through. Built into the bedrock of his principles and expressed in his company's statement of purpose is this notion that all of this is bigger than him and that his goal is the transformation of our industry as a whole:

> *"Our company's purpose is to make the car-buying and servicing experiences pleasurable ones for our customers. In doing so, and leading by example, we will bring integrity and respectability to the image of car dealers everywhere."*

—Stu Stewart

Author's Note: About This Book

For many years now, I have been writing a column for my local weekly newspaper, offering readers insight into the car-buying process. I also host a weekly radio show where my wife, Nancy, and I answer questions from callers about buying and servicing cars.

This book is compiled by category from about 45 of what I thought were my most informative columns.

As you read through these pages, you'll see that the chapters are grouped under six topics: Researching Your New Car, Buying a New Car, Financing a Purchase, Buying a Used Car, Leasing, and Getting Your Car Serviced.

My goal in writing this book is to help you better understand the car-buying and servicing process so you can avoid being taken advantage of by dealers and salespeople who may not always deal with you honestly.

I also hope that by writing this book, I can help all of you become educated consumers, who understand the value of quality customer service and expect excellent customer service in all of your business transactions.

As you read through it, you'll probably notice that certain terms and advice have been repeated more than once, even more than twice. The purpose of this is twofold. The first is to emphasize and reinforce important information.

The second is in case you want or need to know about a particular topic right away before reading the whole book. You can go directly to that topic chapter and find explanations for references mentioned elsewhere that you might need to understand or remember. I hope you will read the whole book, of course, and find it valuable.

Today, I spend a lot of time talking to groups about customer service and the impact it can have on any business. Few people understand this as well as my sons, Stu and Jason — co-general managers — and Josh, our

Internet manager. The result is that, because of our decision to be honest with our customers, we're selling more cars than ever before and running a very profitable dealership.

But more than anything else, by doing right by my customers and by sharing information that I hope will help consumers avoid being taken advantage of by car dealers, I am able to sleep better at night.

Acknowledgements

I would never have had reasons or motivation to write this book were it not for my sons, Stu, Jason, and Josh, and my wife, Nancy. I would have been unable to write this book without Janet Goetz—my comptroller, longest-employed staff member, and very dear friend. Without Janet, I wouldn't have survived all of the hard times we've seen over these last 49 years.

I'm the luckiest father in the world to have three amazingly bright, talented, and hardworking sons who also love our business. Were it not for them, I would have sold my business, retired, and gone fishing a long time ago. And if that doesn't amaze you, how about a wife who also loves the business? Nancy refers more car buyers to us than anybody I know.

Stu was especially helpful in creating this book's cover, proofreading, and selecting and organizing the family pictures. My public relations adviser and friend of more than 25 years, Margie Yansura, was the "wind at my back" for many years, encouraging me to write this book and also helping with the proofreading, and selecting the publisher and editors.

The husband-and-wife communications team, Rich Pollack and Carol Csomay, also helped in bringing the book to fruition. Rich crafted, coordinated, and condensed my five years of monthly blogs and newspaper columns with his expertise as an automotive writer for the *Sun Sentinel,* and Carol, editor for their business, did the final editing and proofreading.

Table Of Contents

Introduction

Section One – Research

Section Two – Buying

Conclusion

Introduction

A new car is, more often than not, the second most expensive item you'll buy in your lifetime, after your home.

Yet it amazes me how few people are as prepared as they should be when they walk into a car dealership.

As a result, people are taken advantage of all the time at car dealerships. How do I know?

Well, because I'm a "recovering car dealer."

I've been in the car business since 1968, and I'm the president of a dealership with roots going back to 1937 when my father opened his Pontiac store in West Palm Beach, Florida.

Today, our Toyota dealership is one of the most successful in Florida, in terms of sales volume and buyer satisfaction, and it is one where many of our customers come back time and time again.

The relationship we have with our customers is based largely on trust — I trust them enough to put my home phone number on my business card and they trust us enough to let us sell them a car.

The truth is, however, that there was a time when customers probably shouldn't have trusted our dealership.

Not all that long ago, we sold cars the old-fashioned way. We used high-pressure haggling techniques, deceptive advertising and some of the "tricks of the trade" — as car dealers like to call them — that immediately gave us an advantage over the customer.

For a number of years now, however, we've been doing things a little differently and we've discovered that it's working even better than before in terms of satisfied customers and total sales.

After reading *Customers for Life*, a book about customer service by Lexus dealer Carl Sewell, and after attending a Toyota management-training program, I came to the conclusion that customers deserve to be treated better and should have all the facts before they buy a car.

A bout with colon cancer a few years ago helped cement that view.

Now, I see things from a different perspective and realize that if you trust your customer, it will help your business grow.

Although it drives my sales crew crazy, I will often meet with customers as they're about to buy a car from us and ask them if they've had a chance to go to the other Toyota dealers in the area and compare prices.

If they haven't, I encourage them to delay buying the car from us until they have. We hope that if they find a better price that they'll bring it to us and give us a chance to beat it.

What we've found is that even when we encourage them to shop around, many customers won't. Instead they tell us that they really like our dealership and want to buy a car from us.

In many ways, our dealership has evolved along with our customers.

Today, my customers are smarter, more affluent, better educated and "nicer." Because I no longer advertise cars for $99 or advertise a car below cost, knowing that there is only one available, I no longer attract customers who are gullible or expecting something for nothing. So I don't attract customers with unrealistic expectations.

With a customer base of buyers who are more knowledgeable about the process, I discover that I don't have lawsuits filed against me by customers, I have the best possible Better Business Bureau rating (A+) and I have employees who enjoy being treated well by customers.

One of the reasons for this book is to help educate consumers so that when they walk into a dealership to make that big purchase or to get their cars serviced, they are better prepared.

Another goal is to help you, the reader, recognize dealerships that don't just talk about customer satisfaction, but that really walk the walk.

Our dealership has been recognized over and over again for our customer service and it starts — as you would expect — at the top.

I strongly believe that a car dealer should always be accessible to customers.

As I mentioned earlier, I give my home phone number to all my customers. When I first started doing this, my wife, Nancy, told me she thought I was out of my mind. She was afraid we would get a lot of phone calls late at night and that customers would not be respectful of our privacy.

The opposite is true, for the most part. We do get an occasional call at home, but there are many weeks when we don't get any.

When I do get calls, I listen carefully to what my customer is saying. By being fully accessible, I am getting valuable insight into what's on the minds of the people who are spending their money with us.

It's something all business owners should do, in the car business and elsewhere.

One of my trademarks, and something we promote heavily, is the use of "hot lines" in the dealership. There are four red phones at our store and when a customer picks one up, it connects to my cell phone.

Our customers won't get a secretary or voice mail—they'll get me. Even if I'm in a meeting, I'll answer the phone when I can.

Another thing that Nancy and I do is to hold periodic meetings with new customers to get to know them and to let them know that we really want to find out what they think.

At our dealership we have "10 Commandments" of customer satisfaction that we ask our staff to follow. They are:

1. Do whatever a customer asks if she believes she is right.

2. Do what is right for the customer even if you don't have to.

3. If your supervisor isn't available, then YOU do what is the right thing for the customer.

4. Always answer all phone calls, emails, texts and messages of any kind from our customers as soon as possible.

5. All customers must be treated with courtesy and respect at all times.

6. Always tell our customers the truth, the whole truth and nothing but the truth.

7. Your first loyalty is to our customers, not to Toyota.

8. You must personally take ownership of our customers' problem.

9. Promise our customers less than you will deliver.

10. Trust your customers as much as you hope they will trust you.

My hope is that as you read through the chapters of this book, you'll become a more educated consumer and have a better understanding of how to find a car dealer you can trust the next time you make that big purchase or bring in your car for service.

Section One

RESEARCH

Chapter 1

Eight Steps to Ensure You Will Be Buying the Best Car for the Best Price

There are many steps you can take before buying a car that can help you find the best one for the best price. This is a brief overview of eight of the most important ones to keep in mind.

1. Check Out *Consumer Reports* Magazine or Website

Subscribe to *Consumer Reports*, go to the library and read past issues or check out *Consumer Reports* online (www.consumerreports.org). There are other objective sources of information on cars, but this is the best.

Consumer Reports accepts no advertising from anybody and the sole goal is to rigorously and objectively test merchandise to help consumers make decisions.

You can very quickly find the best make car for the model and style you want to buy. *Consumer Reports* rates cars by performance, cost of operation, safety and frequency of repair.

2. Test-Drive the Car You Have Chosen

This step requires that you visit a car dealership. Remember that this doesn't have to be the dealership where you'll make your purchase. You obviously must see, touch and drive the car you think you want to buy. A new car is a very personal thing and just because *Consumer Reports* loved it doesn't mean that you will.

Be sure you test-drive the car at all speeds on all road types that you normally drive. Drive it in the city but also on the expressway.

3. Carefully Choose the Accessories You Want

There are some accessories that enhance the value of your car and some that don't, or that may even lower it. Generally speaking, you should accessorize a car comparably to its class.

If you are buying a lower-priced, economy car, you should not load it up with leather seats and an expensive sound system. If you do, you won't recoup much of what you spent on these accessories in its resale value.

On the other hand, if you are buying a luxury car, don't skimp on items people look for in luxury cars, such as a navigation system or moon roof.

4. <u>Carefully Choose Your Car's Color</u>

Believe it or not, color is more important in determining a car's resale value than accessories. To maximize trade-in value, choose one of the most popular colors: white, silver, black or beige, and probably red for sports cars. The difference in trade-in value between the colors can amount to thousands of dollars.

5. <u>Arrange Your Financing</u>

Now that you know exactly what kind of a car you are going to buy, you can check with local banks and credit unions to find the best interest rate. Don't commit until you have chosen the dealer you will buy from. Manufacturers sometimes offer very low special rates and dealers can also sometimes offer a lower rate than your bank or credit union.

6. <u>Shop Your Trade-in</u>

If you are trading in a car, take it to three dealerships selling the same make and ask them how much they will pay you for your car. A Chevrolet dealer will pay more for a used Chevy and a Toyota dealer will pay more for a used Toyota. If you live near a CarMax store, get a price from it, too; it has a reputation of paying more money for trade-ins than most dealers.

Don't commit to the highest bid before giving the dealer you buy from a chance to beat that price. Trading your car in there could save you from paying sales tax.

7. <u>Shop for the Best Price on the Internet</u>

Go to the manufacturer's website. The addresses are all very intuitive. Toyota is www.toyota.com and Chevrolet is www.chevrolet.com. You can type in your ZIP code and get information on all of your local dealers.

Depending on how far you are willing to drive to pick up your new car, request price quotes from as many dealers as you like, but be sure you get at least three.

When you have chosen the lowest price, verify that this price is "out-the-door" with only the cost of taxes and tag added.

8. Offer Your Favorite, or Nearest, Dealer the Right to Meet This Price

If you have been using one dealership for a long time and have had good experiences with its service department, you should give that dealership a chance to meet your lowest Internet price. Of course, you can still take your new car there for service even if you don't buy it there.

You will notice that there were no steps listed above which suggest that you look in your local newspaper's auto classified section, watch car dealers' TV ads or believe their direct mail, too-good-to-be-true offers. When you fall for this, the dealer is in control. When you follow these eight steps, you are in total control.

Read on for more extensive detail on how to do this, as well as what factors can affect the price of the car you want to buy.

Chapter 2

The Internet Price is Usually the Best Price

Ten years from now, I believe that at least 75 percent of all new cars will be purchased over the Internet, even though as of 2011 it was only 15 to 20 percent, according to automotive consulting firm Urban Science. The reason is simply that the Internet price is usually the lowest price and more car buyers are figuring that out every day.

Dealers must give their best prices to prospects inquiring over the Internet because they probably will have only that one chance to sell the car. If they try the "old negotiating game" that usually goes on in a dealership, the Internet prospect will simply choose the lowest price from several other quotes he gets.

When my friends ask me to advise them on how to get the best price on a new car, I always tell them to use the Internet. If they ask me for the best price on my product, Toyota, I give them my Internet price.

I am not suggesting that you not visit your local dealer to see, touch, and drive the new vehicles you are considering. This is very important. You can't make a valid, final decision on which new vehicle is best for you by solely reading data and looking at pictures on the Internet, *Consumer Reports* or any other source. Research of that nature is important, but you should finalize your decision with visits to the dealers to actually experience the vehicle.

Once you have made your final decision on the year, make, model, color and accessories, you are ready to go online and choose the dealer from whom you will buy this specific vehicle. If you are not handy with a computer, ask a friend or relative who is.

First, go to the manufacturer's website, such as www.ford.com, www.toyota.com, www.chevrolet.com, etc. You will be able to type in your ZIP code to find all of the dealers of that make within a given radius, usually about 40 miles, giving you three or four dealers.

To expand the radius, choose another ZIP code near yours.

Websites of the dealers within your radius will come up. Click on their websites and ask for a quote on the specific car you have selected. Most websites have a page for what is called a "quick quote." You type in the year, make, model, color and accessories you're interested in.

It will also ask you for your name, telephone number, address, if you have a trade (check No), whether you are ready to buy now (check Yes) and other questions. All you really need to fill out is year, make, model and accessories and your email address.

If you prefer not to be contacted by phone, don't fill in the phone number. If it's required before you can submit your request, you can type in any 10 digits so that the Web page will allow you to submit it.

If you can't find a quick-quote page, just email your request to the dealer's Internet sales department.

For most of you, this whole process should take less than half an hour. Think of all the time, gasoline, shoe leather and especially aggravation you are saving compared to visiting as many dealerships in person.

The time it will take to get back quotes varies from dealership to dealership. You may get some back within a few minutes, some will take a few hours and some may take a day or two. Believe it or not, some might not respond at all. There are even a few dealers who will not quote a price on the Internet but try to lure you into their store with false promises. Ignore them.

I recommend that you get a minimum of three valid price quotes on your specific vehicle. It's so easy to get quotes, why not get a half dozen or so? You are not necessarily limited by driving distances. If the best price is from a dealer who is too far away, show that quote to a dealer nearer you and ask him if he will match it.

There are some things that you must be careful about. Be sure the price you get is an "out-the-door" price that excludes only federal, state and local fees and taxes, which are usually just for tax and tag.

It also is common for most dealers to tack on a fee of their own, usually referred to as the "dealer fee." These fees vary from around $500 to over $1,000.

This fee is capped and/or highly regulated in many states but not all, for example, here in Florida. So make absolutely sure this fee, which is just profit to the dealer, is included in your out-the-door price. And make sure that no other fees will be added to the price you've been quoted.

Also, be absolutely certain that you are comparing apples to apples. When you select your low bid, double check that this dealer is quoting you on the same year, make, model and accessories as the other dealers.

A good double-check is to compare the MSRP. The MSRP—the manufacturer's suggested retail price—will be identical on identically equipped cars of the same model and year. Also, be sure the car you have gotten the price on will be there when you come in. Give the dealer a deposit on your credit card to hold the car for you.

Internet car buyers are the wave of the future. The retail car business is going through rapid changes and the old-fashioned, price-haggling way of buying cars is slowly but surely becoming obsolete. If you haven't already, now is the time to join the ranks of the smart, sophisticated Internet car buyers.

Chapter 3

Stair-Step Incentives: Why Auto Manufacturers Are Partly to Blame for Dealers' Deceptive Car Pricing

For many years, car manufacturers have employed "stair-step incentives" to motivate their dealers to sell more cars.

A stair-step incentive is bonus money paid directly to dealers to reward them for selling a certain quota of cars within a certain period of time, typically one month. The number of cars in the quota is decided by the manufacturer and is a higher number than the dealer would usually sell.

For example, a dealer who would ordinarily sell 150 cars in one month might be given a quota of 200. If he hits his quota, he earns $250, for example, retroactively on all 200 (or more) cars he sells that month—that is, $50,000 or more. But if he sells only 199 or fewer, he earns nothing extra!

It's easy to understand why this would strongly motivate any car dealer to do whatever it takes to try to sell his quota.

Unfortunately, whatever it takes sometimes translates into "irrational and crazy pricing," the words of Mike Jackson, CEO of AutoNation, the largest retail chain of car dealers in the United States. He spoke before the World Automobile Congress a few years ago and announced that he would make it his mission to end stair-step incentives by auto manufacturers.

At first, one might ask, what's wrong with incentives for a car dealer to sell lots of cars by paying him a large bonus? The answer is that there's nothing wrong with the concept, just with how the concept is applied.

In the example above, the dealer gets $250 per car. If he got $250 every time he sold a car in that month, he would be inclined to discount each car by up to $250.

But the dealer only earns that $250 per car if he sells at least 200 cars and that's more than he would ordinarily sell. You can understand how the very first customer of the month might get a different price from the last customer, especially if the last customer was buying the 200th car!

How can a car dealer tell a customer at the beginning of the month that this is the best price, and give him his best price, when even the dealer doesn't know what he can afford to sell the car for?

On the last day of the month, it's perfectly feasible for a dealer to sell a car thousands below his cost if that's the sale (200th car) that will allow him to hit his $50,000 bonus.

It might seem at first that this can be a great opportunity for the car buyer. Just come in at the end of the month and buy the last car a dealer must sell to hit his quota. This does happen frequently, but the car buyer cannot plan for it any better than the car dealer can.

The dealer may not hit his quota at all or he may have hit it earlier in the month. These stair-step incentives are secret incentives and aren't advertised by the dealer or the manufacturer. In fact, usually even the sales personnel don't know about them. But the managers who control the price that is given to the customer do.

This kind of incentive makes it even more mandatory to do comparison-price shopping.

If you want to buy a new car or truck, you should shop and compare prices with no less than three other dealers of the same make. But you have no way of knowing which dealers will make their stair-step bonus that month.

The dealers who know they have no chance to sell their quota will maintain their normal pricing. Those who are committed to reaching their quota number—and who believe they will—can discount their cars substantially more than the other dealer(s). The dealer who believes he can't hit his quota can give you his lowest price, but it won't be as low as the dealer who will hit his quota.

Stair-step incentives favor larger-volume dealers because they can earn larger bonuses. Imagine two dealers selling the same make of car, the first of whom is a small dealer with a quota of 50 cars while the larger dealer has a quota of 500 cars. The first dealer earns $12,500 when he hits his quota but the larger dealer earns $125,000!

Assume both dealers are stretching to hit their quotas in the last week of the month. Which dealer will likely offer you the best price? It's pretty obvious that the larger dealer can literally give away one or more cars in order to earn his $125,000 bonus.

This sort of thing is why the CEO of AutoNation referred to stair-step incentives as irrational and crazy pricing. And I wholeheartedly agree.

Chapter 4

The Top Ten Advertising Scams

I could write a book just on the top 50 auto ad scams, because the ingenuity for deception in "getting car buyers in the door" is virtually limitless.

However, I chose to concentrate on the 10 most prevalent among South Florida dealers. You can bet, though, that most of them, unless prohibited by law, are just as commonplace all over the country. Be aware as well that there are many more schemes than these I list.

1. Discount from dealer list—Anytime you read or see a car advertised with a large discount, determine whether that discount is from the manufacturer's suggested retail price or the dealer's retail price. There is a difference between the "dealer list price" and the MSRP (manufacturer's suggested retail price). An all-too-common practice is for a dealer to mark up his cars thousands over the MSRP and call it "dealer list" so that he can show huge discounts that aren't real.

2. Prices include "unrealistic" rebates—Manufacturers often offer cash rebates to customers who qualify for special reasons—for example, being on active duty in the U.S. military. This rebate can be as much as $1,500.

If you graduated from an accredited university within the past six months, you can qualify for $500 to $1,000 from some manufacturers.

There is also a customer loyalty rebate which affords you $1,000 or more if you own the same make of car as the one you are buying. There's a similar rebate for lease customers.

There's even a Farm Bureau rebate that qualifies you for hundreds of dollars off if you are a farmer.

Some dealers are actually combining all of these rebates and deducting them from the advertised prices of their cars. Of course, what are the odds that any one customer would simultaneously qualify for all of these rebates? The average reader of these ads probably qualifies for none of them.

3. Lease payments based on large down payments—Virtually every lease payment advertisement requires a large down payment, which is concealed in the fine print. Most people lease because they want to lay out as little cash as possible. If they had $4,000 cash to spend, they would probably opt for a purchase. Those who fall for this trick often end up leasing the car at the full retail price—even though they won't own it at the end of the lease!

Leasing companies—that is, the bank, credit union, finance division or other institution that actually owns the car and to which you make your payments—allow dealers to lease cars for only up to 110 percent of capitalized cost. When you make a down payment, this reduces the net capitalized cost, which allows the dealer to sell your contract to the leasing company.

4. Lowest price guarantee—This guarantee is absolutely worthless. If you read the fine print, you will note that what it essentially says is this: "The dealer reserves the right to buy the car from another car dealer (his competitor) at the same price his competitor quoted you."

"The dealer reserves the right" means that legally the dealer does not have to honor the guarantee if the other dealer refuses to sell him the car at the price the customer was quoted.

Why would any dealer sell his competitor a car at a very low price (probably losing money) so that the competitor could resell the car to his potential customer? No car dealer is going to accommodate his competition so that they can steal away his customer. It's never happened and it never will happen.

Of course, the other fact that makes this guarantee worthless is that it requires that you prove the lower price by presenting a buyer's order from the other dealer signed by a manager.

I know of no car dealer (besides me) who will give a signed copy of the vehicle buyer's order to a customer, unless he drives the car home or makes a substantial, non-refundable deposit.

5. Only one car available at ad price—When you are reading a newspa-

per ad, you will often see a strange number next to the advertised car, for example, STK #T91832. If you are watching the ad on TV or listening on the radio, the number will be unreadable or undecipherable, as is the fine print. This is the stock number of the car and means it is the only car of that model and accessories you can buy at the advertised price.

The ads don't say "only one car available at this price" because you would realize the chance of that car being there (or sold to you if it is there) is very slim.

Don't be misled if the ad also says "many more identical models available at this price."

Here in Florida, the law requires that dealers who charge a dealer fee include it in their advertised price. This applies to all advertising, but if that specific stock number car is unavailable, they can add a dealer fee to the price of an identical car.

This scam is why I continue to lobby the Florida Legislature to require that all profits to dealers be included in all prices, whether verbal or whether advertised in print or on the Internet.

6. Advertised price is "plus dealer-installed accessories"—All this means is that the price you see is not the price you get.

Dealers love to add accessories to their cars because they can set any price they want for them and drastically increase their profit margins. A dealer charging you $299 for pin stripes and floor mats would have a real cost of about $100, allowing him a 300 percent margin.

7. Lease payment based on unrealistically low-mileage allowance—All leasing companies limit the number of miles you can put on their cars without paying a penalty. This is because the higher the mileage, the lower the resale value, and the leasing company always has to sell the car after the end of the lease to make its money back.

The average American drives a car 15,000 miles per year. It's very common with a lease, however, to see mileage limits of 10,000 and even 7,500 miles per year with penalties of 15 to 25 cents per mile over these limits. Under these terms, an average driver in a four-year lease could pay a penalty of $7,500.

The dealers don't get this money—the leasing company does—but the dealers do this so that they can advertise an unrealistically low lease price.

8. Lifetime warranty—Lots of dealers are advertising these "lifetime warranties" on every car they sell. This is a very limited warranty, which applies only to the car's power train. The term power train has different definitions as to which parts of the car it consists of. It typically means only those parts of the engine, transmission, drive shaft and rear axle that are lubricated. These parts virtually never fail, as long as you change your oil as prescribed by the manufacturer or by the issuer of the warranty policy.

If you fail to change your oil as prescribed, the warranty is null and void. It's a win-win for the car dealer. You have to come in to have your car serviced regularly so that he can make more profit and, if you do comply with this, there will never be a claim. Dealers do pay outside warranty companies for these warranties but the cost to the dealer is minuscule, around $25. The low price the dealer pays the warranty issuer is further proof that the warranty is worthless.

9. Purchase payments include a "balloon payment"—How would you like to buy a new BMW 328i for just $339 per month only to discover that your last payment was something close to $12,983! Oh, and you also had to make a down payment of $2,500. Always read the fine print!

10. Internet quotes exclude dealer fee—The average dealer fee in South Florida runs about $850; it can be more or less elsewhere, depending on where dealers are located. As of 2011, 15 to 20 percent of car purchasers were using the Internet to buy cars. Almost 90 percent used the Internet for information about buying their car before going to the dealership.

As an example, here in Florida, almost all car dealers charge a dealer fee and, of these, almost all exclude it from the price you are quoted on the Internet—even though legally they are required to include it.

I recall speaking to a woman who told me she had driven all the way from Lakeland, Fla. to West Palm Beach, Fla.—around 150 miles—to pick up the new Infiniti she had purchased on the Internet. When she got to the dealer, he had added an additional $695 for his dealer fee.

Chapter 5

Buy a Car You Can Afford

I was talking to a friend of mine and I asked her what the one thing was that worried her most about buying a new or used car. She told me that it was paying more for a car than she intended to or could afford.

I always tell people you should know exactly what car you want to buy before you do your comparison shopping. You must also have a firm idea of the most you will pay for that car.

When you begin comparison shopping with these two factors in mind, you are looking for a specific year, make, and model under or at your maximum budgeted price. If you don't find it, go back to the drawing board. Don't buy anything until you have chosen, and comparison shopped for, another car that is exactly what you want at the price you can afford to pay.

When I say, "Know the price you can afford," I am not talking about a monthly payment. Too many people equate price with monthly payments.

In fact, car dealers rely on this confusion to make big profits. If you really want to make a car salesperson's day, just walk into the dealership and say you'll buy that car just as long as she/he can keep your payments under a certain amount.

When you say that, what you are really telling the salesperson is that you don't care about the asking or selling price, whether you buy or lease, what interest rate you pay, what your trade-in allowance is, how well the model you choose retains its value or how long you finance the car.

Each of these items is inextricably tied together and affects the cost of your new car.

Many dealers add a supplementary price sticker alongside the federally mandated Monroney label, which must reveal MSRP, EPA ratings and other information. A dealer's sticker often looks like the Monroney label, and buyers assume it is part of the official MSRP. This extra label adds thousands of dollars to the real retail price suggested by the manufacturer.

Be sure you determine the real MSRP and the real discount from MSRP. In other words, make sure that your discount, let's say it's $2,000, is from the real MSRP on the real Monroney label.

When you lease a car, the leasing company owns the vehicle at the end of the lease, not you. That's why lease payments are so much lower.

When you buy a car, not nailing down the interest rate by competitive shopping allows the dealer to make a lot of money in "finance reserve." This is the money banks pay dealers for charging a premium over the interest rate the bank charges the dealer (the retention rate). The interest profit to the dealer can be thousands of dollars on a single transaction.

If you don't competitively shop your trade-in and check research sources on the Web, the dealer selling you the car might not give you the fair market value for your trade-in, which is just another way of increasing dealer profit.

Some makes and models of cars depreciate faster than others. After three years, some models retain up to 61 percent of their original cost, but some retain as little as 25 percent. This represents a huge price difference between cars that, if you haven't done your research, you probably won't find out about until you trade in that car on your next purchase.

To get some perspective on which cars currently tend to depreciate the most and least, go to the *Kelley Blue Book* (www.KBB.com), consult *Consumer Reports* magazine or visit its website, which may charge a fee for this information.

You can finance a car for 12 months and up to 84 months. The shorter the length of time, the lower the interest cost. Don't be tempted to finance a car for longer than 36 months just to get the payment down.

You can understand why it's not as easy as it sounds to have a firm idea of the most you are willing, or can afford, to pay for a car.

The selling price and monthly payment are just two of seven items that you must have a firm grasp of. There is also leasing or buying, interest rate, trade-in value, resale value of the car you are buying, and length of financing.

If you know only six of the seven, you have left the car dealer a loophole that can cost you money.

Chapter 6

Bait and Switch Advertising: Read the Fine Print

All car dealers pay the manufacturers the same prices for their new cars. Dealers will lead you to believe that volume dealers pay less, but this is not true.

Virtually all of the prices for new cars you see advertised in the newspaper are so low that it would be impossible for a dealer to remain in business if he sold more than a very few cars at that price. The reason for this is that, if a dealer advertised realistic prices with a reasonable profit built in, another dealer need simply advertise a lower price. The dealer who advertises a realistic price is actually helping his competitor sell a car.

Most of the new car prices advertised in the newspaper are below the dealer's actual cost. He protects himself by selling very few at this price and counting this loss as a cost of advertising. Next to an advertised car you will see some letters and numbers, such as #5632A. That is the "stock number" of the car being advertised. This means the dealer has just one vehicle at this price. The chances are that if you are not the first person in the dealership on the morning the ad is in effect, this car will be gone.

Also look for these two fine-print disclosures at the bottom of the ad:

1. Price good on date of publication only.

2. Price good with copy of this ad only.

These are just some more ways a dealer can avoid selling you the car at the advertised price.

Then there are the dealer fees. These fees are really nothing more than additional dealer profits added to the agreed-upon price by most car dealers. They can range from $500 to over $1,000, although some states cap the amount.

The law, at least here in Florida, requires this fee to be included in the advertised price, but often prices are listed without the dealer fee being shown.

When a salesman tells you the advertised car has been sold but he has another one exactly like it, then he can legally add that dealer fee back on.

As you can guess, the salesman's commission on an advertised car can be either zero or very small. Having a very small incentive to sell an advertised car, he will most likely encourage you to buy any other car.

My recommendation to you is to ignore advertised new-car prices. If you must respond to a car ad, call the dealer first and ask if the car is still available. If the answer is no, you have saved yourself a lot of time and aggravation.

If the answer is yes, ask if they will hold the car for you. If you have to, offer to give them your credit card for a deposit to hold the car. If they won't hold the car, save yourself the wasted trip.

As I emphasize throughout this book, the only way to get the best price on a new car is by getting competitive bids from at least three car dealers for the exact same year, make, model, and accessorized car with the identical MSRP.

You can do this on the Internet, by phone or in person. Use *Consumer Reports* magazine, websites—www.edmunds.com and www.kbb.com are two excellent free sources of information—or possibly your local library.

Chapter 7

Should You Buy a Car Through a Broker?

If you aren't familiar with car brokers, they are third parties, mostly individuals but sometimes companies, who act as intermediaries between you and the car dealer, supposedly to get you a better price than you would be able to obtain by yourself.

Most dealerships, including mine, deal with brokers. The dealer pays virtually all brokers a fee and some also charge the customers a fee — a "double dip" you might say.

The fees the brokers charge range all over the map. I don't remember paying a broker less than $500 and have paid up to $5,000. Charges to the customers range from $250 to $750. If the broker is charging you a fee, you can be almost certain he is also charging the dealer at least as large a fee.

Another way brokers do business is to actually buy the car and then sell it to you. To do this they must have a dealer license; otherwise they would have to pay sales tax on the transaction.

Buying the car allows them to mark up the car to you as their compensation and they may charge you a fee on top of that.

As you can see, the price of going through a broker raises the price of the car you buy. The only question is does it raise the price above what you could pay by purchasing the car directly?

The answer to this question depends entirely on your buying skills. If you are of at least average intelligence and follow the advice that I've given in this book, you should be able to buy most cars from a dealer at as low a price as a broker can obtain for you.

This means you will save anywhere from $500 to $5,000 in fees that you don't have to pay. I don't care what a broker may tell you, a dealer will always sell you the car at just as low a price as he charges a broker, if you are a skilled buyer and do your homework.

Of course, there are reasons other than price that car buyers seek brokers.

As I've often said, buying a car can be a very unpleasant experience.

If you go about buying a car the right way, though, you minimize the unpleasantness. Don't ever go into a dealership without doing your homework about the exact year, make and model you want, accessorized exactly as you wish. Always get at least three competitive prices.

If at all possible, do your shopping in the comfort of your home on the Internet. If you're not cyber savvy, ask for help from a friend, son, daughter or grandchild who is. You can get your best car price that way without ever having to leave your house.

It stands to reason that you'll save yourself a lot more time, not to mention aggravation, if you aren't on the phone or out visiting dealers searching for the same information you can get on the Internet.

Two excellent websites you can consult are www.kbb.com (*Kelley Blue Book*) and www.edmunds.com. They have vast amounts of free information on dealer cost, quality ratings, trade-in values, etc.

A lot of people rely on their credit unions for advice on which dealer from whom they should buy a car. It sounds like a good idea because credit unions handle thousands of these transactions and have experience with lots of car dealers.

I must warn you, though, that there are employees in credit unions who are paid fees by car dealers—which essentially are not any different from a broker's fee—for referrals.

Also, many credit unions sell extended warranties on cars they finance and may refer you to dealers who have agreed not to sell you their extended warranty. This is a potential conflict of interest.

So, if you use a referral from your credit union, be sure to get prices from at least two other dealers as well.

If you are accustomed to going through a broker to buy your cars, I suggest that on your next purchase, you also get prices directly from two other dealers as well. Compare those prices with your broker's price and be sure you don't pay him a fee unless you buy the car through him.

Chapter 8

An Open Letter to Auto Dealers: Eliminate the Dealer Fee

This chapter stems from a newspaper column I wrote several years ago as an open letter to car dealers in Florida to encourage them to drop their dealer fees. I've updated the letter, but my feelings about this have not changed a bit since then; I still believe it is a very important issue.

While this was specifically directed to Florida dealers, it also applies to dealers in other states.

I started in the retail auto business in 1968 and I've seen a lot of changes in the way we dealers sell cars and in the expectations of our customers.

Many car dealers add a charge to the price of the cars they sell, variously referred to as a dealer fee, documentary fee, dealer prep fee, etc. This extra charge is printed on the buyer's orders.

This is allowed here in Florida, as well as most other places around the country, although it is strictly regulated and severely limited in many states, including capping the amount dealers can charge.

I stopped charging this fee in 2004. Since then, I'm happy to say that the other Toyota dealerships in Palm Beach County, where I have my dealership, have also dropped their dealer fees, along with those in adjacent Martin County to the north.

The truth, though, is that almost all of you who can do so will attempt to charge a dealer fee, or another fee disguised as one, to every customer—and it ranges from a few hundred dollars to $1,000 or more.

Florida law requires that you disclose, in writing on the buyer's order, that this charge represents profit to the dealer.

You must also include this fee in all advertised prices. But you dealers don't always do this. One way you get around this law is by limiting the number of advertised vehicles to as few as one.

The argument I hear from most car dealers when I raise this issue is that the dealer fee is fully disclosed on the buyer's order.

But most car buyers are totally unaware that they are paying this. Who reads all of the voluminous paperwork associated with buying a car?

The few who notice it generally assume it is an official fee, such as a state sales tax or a license and registration fee.

Those astute buyers who do question the fee are told that your dealership must charge this fee on every car if they charge anyone, which is not true.

These same buyers are also told that all other car dealers charge similar fees. This is almost true, but as I stated, my dealership, along with a few others, does not.

The reason you charge this fee is simply to increase the cost of the car and so increase the profit in such a manner that it isn't noticed by the customer.

Some of you will admit this to me in private conversations and also that you have considered eliminating the fee, but are afraid of the drastic effect on your bottom line.

By being able to count on an extra $895 or more in profit that your customer is not aware of or believes is an official fee, you can actually quote a price below cost and end up making a profit.

Or, if the price quoted to the customer does include a nice profit, you can then increase that by several hundred dollars.

This extra, unseen profit is even better for you because you don't pay your salesmen a commission on it. That's being unfair to your employees as well as to your customers.

When the rare, astute buyer objects to the dealer fee, you can decrease the quoted price of the car by the amount of this fee, which would have the same effect as removing it. This would protect you from any liability as to discrimination in pricing.

But your salespeople don't want to agree to it because they would lose their commission (typically 25 percent) on the decrease in their commissionable gross profit.

I should tell you that I don't profess to be some holier-than-thou car dealer who is always perfect. Although I never did anything illegal, when

I look at some of my advertising and sales tactics 20-plus years ago, I am not always proud. But, I have evolved as my customers have evolved.

My customers' expectations and levels of education and sophistication are much higher today. Your customers are no different. As I began treating my customers, and employees, better, I discovered that they began treating me better.

Yes, I used to charge a dealer fee ($495), and when I stopped charging it, it was scary. But I did it because I could no longer, in good conscience, mislead my customers. Just because everybody else was doing the same thing did not make it right.

Now, here is the good news. My profit per car did drop by about the amount of the dealer fee when I stopped charging it. But, when my customers realized that I was now giving them a fair shake and quoting the complete out-the-door price with no surprises, the word spread. My volume began to rise rapidly.

Sure, I was making a few hundred dollars less per car — but I was selling a lot more cars. I was, and am, selling to a lot of your former customers. My bottom line is far better than it was when I was charging a dealer fee. You can do the same.

I don't think of myself as the new marshal that has come to clean up Dodge. In fact, I am well aware that this message may appear self-serving. A lot of people will read this and learn why they should buy a car from me, not my competition.

And, I am also aware that most dealers who read this will either get angry and ignore it or not have the nerve to follow my lead.

But maybe you will be the exception. If you should take this message to heart and decide to drop your dealer fee, you will be doing your customers, your employees and yourselves a big favor. And – you will also be doing the right thing.

Chapter 9

The Lowest-Priced Car Can End Up Being the Most Expensive

Too often car buyers focus on buying the car that fulfills their preferences of styling, size and accessories that they can buy for the lowest price. There are other important cost considerations you should look at before buying the cheapest alternative.

Resale value is the No. 1 consideration that is most often overlooked by car buyers. All cars depreciate in value, but some hold their value a lot better than others.

You might save one thousand dollars by choosing to buy one used or new car over another more expensive make and model. But if the make and model that cost $1,000 more held its value by $2,000 more over the three years you owned the car before trading it back in, then the "lowest priced car" was really $1,000 more expensive.

There are several ways you can check on how much cars will depreciate. A good one is to check the resale value of that same make of car that is three or four years old. You can do that with a wholesale buying guide such as *Kelley Blue Book, NADA Appraisal Guide* or *Black Book.* You can also find this information on the Internet.

If you are thinking about buying a new car, find out what a 2-year-old car of that model and make sells for today. Compare other makes and models.

Maintenance and repair costs are the second-biggest factors in measuring the true cost of a car. When a car has a relatively higher depreciation, one of the biggest reasons is because it is probably more prone to breaking down.

Check *Consumer Reports* or go online to find the projected repair histories of the cars you are comparing. Saving $1,000 on a particular make and model is not very significant when you are facing the cost of a blown transmission or engine.

Big cash rebates and big discounts are not necessarily a good thing. First you have to ask yourself, why is it necessary for this manufacturer to be giving me such a big cash rebate (I have seen them advertised as high as $11,000) to sell this car?

You will generally find that the manufacturers of higher quality, higher-demand cars offer fewer rebates and discounts. These are also the manufacturers of cars that depreciate less and cost less in repairs. In addition, big rebates and discounts negatively affect a car's resale value.

It's what you could call a vicious cycle. A car is hard to sell because of its high repair costs and high depreciation, so the manufacturer pays a big cash rebate to sell it. The rebate lowers the value of the used car of that make and model because the price of a used car is directly tied to the cost of that same new car.

You will be surprised how much the color of the car you buy can affect the resale value. Think about it. The color was very important to you when you bought your last car. It is just as important to the person who will be buying the car you trade in.

The most popular colors are white, silver, beige and black. If you have a thing for green, blue, orange or another unusual color, it can negatively affect the resale value of that car by more than $2,000.

I'm not suggesting that you always buy neutral colors, but if you like them, you are going to get more money for that trade-in than if you opt for blue or green. Bright colors can be popular for certain models, however, such as red for a convertible.

Be sure to check your cost of insurance before you make a final decision. Cars with side air bags, highly rated in collision and rollover tests, relatively low cost of repair—especially for bumpers—and non-high-performance cars have much lower insurance rates.

Cars are no different from any product that you buy when it comes to the principle of "the cheapest product is usually not the best value." You buy a quality pair of shoes—paying more than you would for a cheap, poorly made pair—because they will look good and wear many times longer.

Shopping for the lowest price is a very good idea, but only after you have chosen a car that has low depreciation, operating costs and cost of repair.

Chapter 10

Don't Get Shafted

Here are 10 things to commit to memory when buying a new car:

1. Don't Believe Newspaper and TV Ads

It never ceases to amaze me how outrageous and unbelievable car dealers' claims are. Just when I think that they can't get any worse, I see one that tops them all. One dealer advertised in the newspaper and on TV that if you bought one vehicle from him you got a second one for nothing. The "facts and fine print" would reveal that the first vehicle was a very expensive one with a huge markup of more than $6,000 and the second vehicle was only the "use" of one for two years—in other words, a lease.

My father always said, "If it sounds too good to be true, it probably is" (too good to be true). Astoundingly, the general manager of this dealership had the gall to say on TV, "This is not a gimmick."

2. Don't Buy a Car on Impulse on the First Day You Start Shopping

Can you believe that this is the way most people buy cars? It truly is. There is something about a new car that excites people and appeals to them on an emotional level. People let their feelings short circuit their logical thought processes. Overcome any emotion that tells you that you must drive home a shiny new car right now.

Go home and think about it. Talk it over with your spouse and friends. Research the model of car you looked at and the price on the Internet, especially if you haven't already done so.

Always drive the car you chose before you sign any papers. You should take at least a week or two in the decision-making process before you buy a car.

3. Don't Trade Your Old Car in to the Dealer You Buy from Without Shopping its Value

Most people have no idea what their trade-in is worth when they come in to buy a new car. They rely entirely on the appraisal by the selling dealer. The dealer can make it appear that he is giving you a lot of money for your trade by taking some of the high markup on the new car and showing it as part of the appraisal value. Check *Kelley Blue Book* (kbb.com) and Edmunds.com on the Internet to get a perspective on your trade-in's value.

Get at least three bids from other dealers of the same make for your trade. Make the purchase of the new car and the sale of your trade two separate transactions. But remember, in some states like Florida, you do get a sales tax break by trading in your car to the dealer from whom you buy.

4. Don't Use the Dealer's Financing Without Checking with Your Bank or Credit Union

Shop for the best price on your financing just as you would shop for the best price on your trade-in and the best price on your new car.

5. Don't Believe This: "This Low Price is Good Today Only"

This is one of the favorite ruses used by car sales people and dealers. In 99 percent of the cases, you can buy that car for the same or an even lower price later. The only time that you can't is when factory incentives expire on a certain date, typically at the end of the month. If that is the claim, demand to see the written factory incentive by the manufacturer.

6. Don't Fall for This: "Make Me a Written Offer with a Deposit and I Will Submit it to My Manager"

This is S.O.P. (standard operating procedure) at most car dealerships to get you psychologically engaged in the buying process. Once you have signed a buyer's order and written out a deposit check, chances are you will remain in the dealership for a while and are more likely to buy. The salesman knows that.

Insist on getting the dealership's best price on the car you have selected. You should never make the first offer. Once you have that price, compare it with at least three other prices from other dealers on the same make and model.

7. Don't Follow this Advice: "Take this New Car Home and See How You Like it"

This is the famous "puppy dog" technique, so named because once you take a puppy dog home overnight, who has the heart to return it the next day? You, your neighbors and friends will see that shiny new car parked in your driveway. It sure looks good. How are you going to explain to anybody that you didn't buy it?

8. Don't Negotiate this Way: "I'll Buy the Car if You can Get My Monthly Payments Below $X"

Most of us tend to think in terms of our monthly budgets. We might feel that we can afford a new car as long as it costs us less than $350 per month. But there is a big difference between $350 per month for 36 months and $350 per month for 72 months. I recommend that you finance a car for no more than 42 months, preferably 36.

9. Don't Believe the Salesman when he Says: "You Have My Word On That"

Be absolutely sure that every promise or commitment made to you by your salesperson is in writing and signed by a manager. That salesman may not still work there when you have occasion to ask for that free loaner car he promised you anytime you bring your car in for service.

10. Don't Fall for this: "All Dealers Charge a Dealer Fee and We Can't Remove it from the Invoice"

In some states dealer fees are capped and carefully regulated, but in fact, even in those states where they aren't, there are a few dealers who do not charge this fee. I don't.

But unfortunately, most of them do charge this "gotcha" fee ranging from $500 to over $1,000. There is no reason for charging this fee other than additional profit to the dealer.

It is true that Florida, as well as some other states, requires that a dealer fee must appear on all invoices; it is my opinion that Florida should prohibit dealer fees entirely.

In addition, if dealers charge just one customer a dealer fee, they are advised by legal counsel, at least in Florida, to charge all their customers a dealer fee.

It seems that some lawyers, in their infinite wisdom, decided if car dealers are going to take advantage of even one buyer, they must take advantage of all of their buyers—never discriminate.

But there is a loophole for consumers in this stupid law. You can, and should, demand that the dealer reduce the price of the car by the amount of the dealer fee, making it a wash.

Chapter 11

Caveat Emptor:
Let the Buyer Beware

Almost everyone has heard the popular saying often attributed to Abraham Lincoln, "You can fool some of the people all of the time, and all of the people some of the time, but you can't fool all of the people all of the time."

I think Abe meant this to be a positive assertion that government may get away with deceiving us for a while, but in the long run, truth, justice and the American way will prevail, and I think he was right.

However, it doesn't work that way with unethical car dealers and car buyers. It always has been caveat emptor, or "Let the buyer beware," when it comes to buying or servicing a car.

Unfortunately, for a buyer to beware he must be aware, that is to say, educated, mature, sophisticated and experienced. This excludes a very large segment of our population, including the very young, the very old, the uneducated, those with low IQs and those not proficient in the English language.

Is this one reason why our regulators and politicians don't seem to care or take action with respect to the rampant unfair and deceptive sales practices of a large number of car dealers?

Many elected officials and regulators are lawyers and are highly educated and sophisticated. They don't have a problem buying or servicing a car. In fact, the car dealer who tries to take advantage of a lawyer, regulator or politician is asking for trouble.

Unfortunately, there are enough uneducated, naive and otherwise vulnerable consumers to feed those unethical car dealers who prey on the defenseless among us. All you have to do is read some of the car ads in the Saturday (the biggest selling day for most car dealers) auto classifieds.

To the educated, sophisticated buyer, these ads are actually funny if you can forget the fact that so many people fall prey to them and are taken advantage of by dealers.

For example, it's hard for you or me to believe that anybody would respond to an advertisement without reading the fine print. Many dealers today are advertising prices that, when you read the fine print, are understated by thousands of dollars. When you or I see a dealer stating that the car price is plus freight, we are educated enough to understand that the law requires that the freight cost must already be included in the price.

A shrewd buyer knows that "dealer list price" is not the same thing as the manufacturer's suggested retail price (MSRP) and that a large discount from "dealer list" means absolutely nothing.

There are those who argue all buyers have the responsibility to guard against unethical sellers, to take care of themselves.

That sounds good, but what about the elderly widow whose husband recently died and who never had to make a decision on a major purchase in her entire life? What about the young person just out of school with no experience in the real world? How about the immigrant who struggles with English?

You and I know lots of good people who, for one reason or another, simply can't cope with a slick car or service salesman.

My bottom line is this: Since we can't rely on our regulators and politicians to protect those who "can be fooled all of the time," maybe we owe it to society to protect these folks.

If you know someone who is thinking about buying a car or has a car service problem and you feel he or she may not have the ability to fend for himself or herself with the car dealer, offer your support. If you're one of the people who needs support, ask someone who can go "toe to toe" with a car dealer to come with you when you are car shopping.

Nobody, sophisticated or not, should car shop alone. Two heads are always better than one and it's always a good idea to have a witness to what was said during a negotiation.

Chapter 12

Buy or Lease Your New Car at the Right Time of the Year

The total cost of a new car consists of many factors, including purchase price, maintenance and repairs and insurance.

One of the most often overlooked and biggest costs of owning a car, though, is depreciation. Some makes and models of cars depreciate more quickly than others. By choosing the right make and model you can minimize depreciation.

You can also minimize depreciation by properly maintaining your car, protecting it from the elements and selecting the best color. The one important factor in depreciation that is most often overlooked, however, is the time of year that you buy or lease your car.

You should always buy your new car as soon as possible after that year model is introduced.

Some would disagree, arguing that you can buy a car for less at the end of the model year. Even if this were so (and I don't agree that it is), the savings would not offset the increased cost of depreciation that you inherit by buying a new car that is a year old.

If you follow the advice I have given in my previous chapters on the smartest way to buy a new car, you can usually buy one for close to the same price at the beginning of the model year as at the end.

There was a time when virtually all makes of cars were introduced in the last quarter of the calendar year preceding the model year. If you bought a new model in September, you could be assured that you got it at the right time of year to minimize your depreciation.

Nowadays, new models are introduced at almost anytime, and the timing of the introductions is nearly unpredictable. It's not unheard of for a manufacturer to actually skip a model year entirely, selling last year's model for another year. Or, sometimes a manufacturer will introduce a new model as much as two years before the calendar date of that model year.

You should check online sites such as www.edmunds.com to learn exactly when the model year you contemplate buying was introduced. You don't want to buy a model year that was introduced six or eight months ago.

If you are leasing your car, you should also try to lease it as soon as possible after that year model is introduced. Also, when deciding on the length of the lease, your lease should end when the new model that you will lease or buy next will be introduced.

You don't have to lease a car for exactly one, two, three or four years. You can lease a car for 39 months, for example, which may assist you in having your lease terminate at just the right time to buy or lease your next car.

You should try to find out as much as you can about how many more years the make and model you select will remain before it is replaced by a major model change. But even dealers don't always know.

This information is closely guarded by the manufacturers — dealers often aren't notified until just before the production of that model has begun. Also, dealers are given a pretty broad range of time as to when to expect the new models, like "early spring" or "fourth quarter." It's not definitive.

The life cycle of a particular model varies between manufacturers from as short as three years to as long as six or seven years.

Your car will retain its value considerably if it is still within its current product cycle when you trade it in. You need to be especially wary when a specific model is discontinued entirely; in other words, if you know that a car is going to be discontinued, you probably don't want to buy it.

Research this carefully and time your purchase or lease as early in the product cycle as possible.

If you are buying a brand new model at the beginning of its product cycle, be sure it is from a manufacturer that has a very good reputation for quality.

You can get a pretty good idea of the quality of the new model by researching the reliability of the previous year's model. It is true that a brand new model can experience some bugs during the early months of its first year. If you are nervous about this, it might pay to wait for three or four months after a new model is introduced to see if problems in the form of recall campaigns or other problems occur.

Section Two

BUYING

Chapter 13

Emotion is Your Enemy When Buying a Car, But Your Dealer's Emotion Can Be Your Friend

It's hard to believe, but a high percentage of people will buy a new or used car on the first day they go car shopping.

Many buyers never even compare prices with other dealers or research the car for safety, fuel economy, reliability, maintenance costs or resale value.

I always advise people that their car-purchase process should take weeks. You must not only choose the best car to meet your needs, but you must choose the best price by getting at least three competitive quotes. The best price must include your trade-in and your financing interest rate.

But there's another strategy you might want to consider as well. Did you know that emotion can be the car dealer's enemy sometimes and that this can work to your benefit?

There are two forces that have the net effect of driving car dealers and their salesmen and managers into an emotional frenzy. One is the end of the month and the other is the "stair-step" incentive system.

It might sound like an old wives' tale or an urban legend to be debunked by Snopes (www.snopes.com, an Internet reference source that verifies or dispels rumors, questionable stories, etc.), but car dealers almost always do sell cars for less at the end of a month. This is for a variety of reasons including:

- Dealers and manufacturers concentrate their advertising of sales and specials in the second half of the month.

- Manufacturers' and dealers' rebates and incentives typically expire at the end of the month.

- Salesmen and sales managers are usually paid bonuses, which culminate at the end of the month. Salesmen are paid volume bonuses and just one car sale can mean $1,000 or more on the last day of the month.

- Manufacturers live for market share and sales numbers are widely publicized at the end of each month. Ford wants to outsell GM; Honda wants to outsell Toyota, etc.

- Stair-step incentives are the most popular way that manufacturers motivate dealers to sell more cars. For example, a dealer can earn a $500 incentive for each car sold in a given month but not until he sold the number of cars in his objective set by the manufacturer, say 250 cars.

If the dealer sells 249 cars in the month, he earns zero incentive money. If he sells 250, he earns $125,000!

Now, I think you can understand why you, a customer for that 250th car at midnight on the last day of the month, might be able to negotiate a pretty good price. In fact, it would actually pay the dealer to give you the car.

Of course, it isn't only the 250th buyer but all buyers that the dealer believes may help him hit his objective. At the beginning of the month, it's too soon to know if a particular sale will be the pivotal one.

Depending on when during the month you're reading this, say, for example, the beginning of April, you could have as much as three or four weeks before the end of the month to do your homework and choose the right car. You have plenty of time to get three prices on the car you want to buy, as well as on your trade-in and financing.

Now the fun part is to wait until the last day of the month and visit the dealer who gave you the lowest price earlier in the month. There's a very good chance that you can negotiate a better price by hundreds, if not thousands, of dollars.

Your emotions can be the enemy when you buy a car but the dealer's emotions can be your friend.

Chapter 14

Never Go Car Shopping Alone

I remember a letter a woman wrote to me in response to one of my newspaper columns.

Her husband had recently passed away and this was the first car she had bought on her own.

The dealer did not have the model car with the accessories she wanted and was unable to locate one at another dealership. She did not want to make a decision without seeing the actual car she wanted to purchase, but the salesman and manager talked her into signing a buyer's order, assuring her that she was under no obligation to buy.

They also included two accessories that she did not want because "the manufacturer required it."

I've heard of distributors ordering cars with certain accessories from the manufacturer—which essentially makes them standard—but never a $250 set of floor mats, which was one of the accessories for which she was charged!

I get a lot of emails, phone calls and letters from people who've made a bad deal with their car purchase and want to know how they can get out of it. This example is actually one of the less egregious I've heard, but I chose it because it was simple to explain.

There is strength in numbers when shopping and negotiating to buy a car. In fact, this applies to any serious decision in life. You might be the sharpest, shrewdest negotiator on the block, but your odds of striking a better deal and not getting taken advantage of are enhanced when you have others on your side.

Personally, I make a habit of always having at least one partner when I am engaged in a serious, adversarial decision-making process. When meeting with those on the other side, I make it a point to arrive with at least as many people as they have present. One reason is the psychological factor. When you are in an office by yourself with two or three others, it can be intimidating.

Another reason is that you always have people on your side to corroborate what was said. If a salesman or a sales manager makes a verbal promise that can be corroborated by a friend or two, it is far less likely to be broken. It will also hold up in court if it has to come to that. Of course, the better solution is to see that all promises are committed to in writing.

Buying a car, especially a new car, is, more often than not, an emotional decision. Having a friend or two with you can help you make more of an analytical, logical one.

Another point of view is always useful when making an important decision. Also, having one or two friends with you slows down the process to a level more easily absorbed and understood by you. A friend will often think of a question you should have asked but forgot.

Ideally, you should bring someone with you who is skilled in negotiation and experienced in buying cars. However, if you don't know somebody like that, anyone is better than no one.

By the way, most car dealers aren't happy when prospective customers bring in advisers and friends. Naturally they feel that way because they recognize their chances of making a fast, very profitable sale are diminished.

Chapter 15

Answers to the Top 10 Devious Statements Made by Car Salesmen

A car salesman might try to pressure you into buying a car. Here are 10 devious statements and the responses you might want to give:

1. "I'll give you the price only if you'll commit to buy today."

Your answer: "I'll ask you once more for your best price. There are three car dealerships that sell this same make within a half-hour's drive of here. If I don't get your best price right now, I'll walk out of your showroom and you'll never see me again."

2. "I'm sorry. We just sold that car we advertised but we have others just like it."

Your answer: "If you do not sell me the car I came in to buy, for the advertised price, I will walk out that door and you will never see me again."

3. "This price is good for today only."

Your answer: "I want to shop and compare your price with your competition and, if yours is the best price, I will call you to see if I can buy it for that price. If you tell me that I can't, I'll buy it from your competitor."

4. "This price is so low, that I'm willing to guarantee it or pay you $1,000 (or some other amount) if you can find a better one."

Your answer: "First of all, no retailer can always have the lowest prices. If you did, you could not make a profit and remain in business. I'll bet you can't give me the name of just one customer that you paid your $1,000 guarantee to. I also know that you reserve the right to buy the exact car from the dealer that I say has the lower price.

"What makes you think that I would believe your competitor would sell you that car so that you could steal his customer? You must think I'm really stupid and I don't want to buy a car from salespeople who think their customers are stupid."

5. "I can give you this price only if you take a car from my present inventory. If I have to order a car or dealer-trade a car, the price will be higher."

Your answer: "My car is very important to me. I want the exact color and accessories that will satisfy me and not a compromise. I will buy the car from you only if you agree to get me the exact car I want at the price you just quoted me. If not, I'll bet that your competitor will."

6. "I can't give you this price in writing unless you will give me a deposit."

Your answer: "I know that you may be allowed to keep my deposit if I change my mind about buying. I also know that you do not want to commit to a price in writing because I might show your price to your competitor who may beat it. That's the risk you have to take if you want my business. If you do, you have a chance at my buying a car from you. If you don't, you have no chance because you will never see me again."

7. "What will you pay for this car today? Make me an offer on this car and I'll take it to my manager for approval."

Your answer: "This is not a game that we're playing. I'm about to make the second-largest purchase of my life. If I were shopping for a TV set and the salesman said that to me, I would walk out without another word and buy from his competitor. And that's exactly what I'm about to do to you unless you give me your best price in writing."

8. "We cannot quote you a price over the phone."

Your answer: "It makes no sense to me that I should have to drive 10 miles to your dealership and back just so that you can tell me the price of the car I want to buy. I can get prices on the Internet so why can't I get them on the telephone?

"I think the reason you want me to drive to your dealership is so that you can pressure me into buying today, without competitive shopping. If you won't give me your best price right this minute, you will never hear from me again because I will buy from your competitor."

9. "I'm sorry but the owner isn't available right now and we are not allowed to give out his cell phone number."

   Your answer: "If the owner of this dealership is too busy to speak to
his customers, then I'm too busy to buy my next car from him."

10. "The reason that this $749 item labeled dealer fee (or doc fee, dealer
prep, handling fee, administration fee, pre-delivery fee, etc.) was not
included in the price that I quoted you is because its purpose is to cover
our costs of inspecting, cleaning and adjusting vehicles, and preparing
documents for sale."

   Your answer: "The price quoted to a customer for any product should
include all of the costs of the seller.

   "Furthermore, I know that the manufacturers of all cars reimburse
their dealers for inspecting, cleaning and adjusting vehicles. I also know
that now you're going to tell me that you must charge me your dealer fee
because you charge all customers this same fee. But I also know that you
can deduct the amount of that fee from the price you quoted me and
leave the dealer fee on the buyers' order, which will have the net effect of
removing it. If you do not agree, I will walk out of your dealership and
never return."

Chapter 16

Holdback is Holdup for Consumers

Back in 1968, when I first went into the retail car business with my father, I can remember asking him, "What is holdback?"

I was learning the business and had been studying the invoices on new Pontiacs that General Motors sent us when they shipped a new car that we had ordered. We had to pay the invoice immediately when it was issued, sometimes even before the car arrived at our dealership. Actually, in most cases, it was our bank or GMAC who paid GM, and we borrowed the money from there to pay for the car.

My father's answer to my question about holdback was that it was an increase in the amount of the invoice that we paid General Motors, which was not really part of the price of the car, and which would be returned to us. It was just an extra amount added to the real price of the car and included in the invoice.

At that time, it was 2 percent of MSRP (manufacturers suggested retail price), so if a new Pontiac Bonneville had an MSRP of $10,000 and a true cost of $9,000, the factory invoice would be $9,200.

I asked my father, "When do we get the $200 back?" He said, "At the end of the year." I asked him if they paid us interest on our money and I can remember him laughing loudly and saying no.

Of course, my next question was, "Why would they do that?" He told me the reason they gave him was to help dealers sell their cars for more money so that they didn't go broke. He said because dealers didn't get their holdback money for such a long period of time, they began to think of the invoice as being the actual cost of the car.

General Motors felt that many dealers were such poor businessmen they might sell their cars so cheaply they would go out of business. Now, because GM was kind enough to hold back hundreds of thousands of the dealers' money (and pay them no interest on it) but return the money to them once a year, they could help the dealers make a bigger profit and maintain adequate working capital.

At that time, I thought this was the biggest bunch of baloney I had ever heard and was sure this was a scheme by manufacturers to keep a free float of millions of their dealers' money under the guise of helping them.

I asked my father why the dealers didn't strongly object to this and he said that most dealers actually liked the idea of holdback. When I heard that, I thought that maybe GM and the manufacturers were right about the dealers not being smart enough to sell their cars for a reasonable profit.

It took me a few more years in the business before I understood what was really going on with holdback. It was a no-brainer as to why the manufacturers liked it, but at last I understood its attraction to us dealers.

My father was right. Because we had to pay an extra amount over the true price of the car and not see that money for up to a year, we really would begin to think of the invoice as the true price, even though it was actually inflated by hundreds of dollars.

Because all manufacturers added holdback to all dealers' invoices, the net effect was to raise the price of all cars to all buyers by the amount of this holdback.

I know this is a dirty word, but it is price fixing on the grandest of scales. This might have been something that Henry Ford, Alfred Sloan and Walter Chrysler concocted while playing golf at Bloomfield Hills Country Club outside of Detroit.

Another neat thing about holdback for dealers is being able to tell our customers that we are only charging them "X dollars over invoice." Or, we can tell them that we will sell them this car at invoice with no profit to us at all. ("There's a sucker born every minute," as the saying goes.)

Dealers often have "invoice sales" with copies of the invoice pasted on the car windows. Who doesn't believe that an invoice is the cost of the car? The truth is in the semantic skullduggery: "Mr. Customer, I solemnly swear to you that this the exact price that I paid the factory for this car. In fact, here's a copy of the invoice."

That's what the dealer "paid" the factory all right, but it's not what he paid the factory after he got his holdback check in the mail.

You might be thinking, so we're talking about $200 more or less on a $10,000 car. Who cares? That was more than 40 years ago. Holdbacks have expanded considerably and now, instead of several hundred dollars, we're talking several thousand.

Also, dealers no longer have to wait a year to get their holdback money returned. Now they get it back monthly. Manufacturers have even changed the name of these monies they hold back, innocuous so that if you see the invoice, you will have no suspicions. These are names like floor plan assistance, advertising, PDI, administrative or DAP.

Of course, there are also cash rebates to dealers that don't show on the invoice. I estimate the average car invoice today includes $1,500 to $4,000 in hidden holdbacks to the dealer. Holdbacks are also applied to factory or distributor accessories, such as "protection packages" (wax, undercoat, window etch, roadside assistance), floor mats, window tint, etc.

The bottom line is: Don't rely on the dealer's factory invoice to determine the price you are willing to pay for a car. And be especially suspicious when the dealer quotes you a price of X dollars over invoice or actually shows you the invoice.

You've heard the old joke: "How can you tell when a politician is lying?"

Answer: "When his lips are moving."

Consider this question: "How can you tell when a car dealer is lying?"

Answer: "When he shows you the factory invoice."

Chapter 17

Rules of Negotiating

Buying a new or used car is one of the last bastions of the negotiated price.

In some countries, negotiation is fairly commonplace in retail stores, but in America virtually all products are sold at a fixed price. Some of us are simply not comfortable negotiating and most of us are not very good at it.

As I have said previously, the best way to buy a new or used car is on the Internet. You can do your research on which car is the best to suit your needs, get guidance on what kind of price you can expect to pay and get quotes from several dealerships on that specific car. However, everybody is not Internet savvy and if you are not, or for a number of other reasons, you might find it necessary or desirable to visit a car dealership and negotiate for the lowest price.

If you are not comfortable with negotiation, the best advice I can give you is to bring someone along who is. Car salespeople and sales managers are trained experts in negotiation. This is how they make their living.

Here are some tips for you if you decide that you want to negotiate the best price on a car:

1. If you have a trade-in, keep that separate from the negotiation. Negotiate the best price on the car you are buying and then negotiate the best price you can get for your trade-in.

2. Don't fall for the old "over allowance on your trade-in" ruse. This is when the dealer marks up the price of the car you are buying higher so he can make you think you are getting more for your trade-in.

3. Never buy a car based on payments alone. Always negotiate the best price you can for the car you are buying and then calculate your best payment when you have negotiated for the best interest rate.

4. Be sure you understand how the dealer arrived at his retail price. Federal law dictates that a Monroney label—the standard label on every new car with the new price listing and EPA rating—be affixed with a manufacturer's suggested retail price to every vehicle.

Many dealers mark up that price with another label, often referred to as a "market adjustment addendum." This markup can be several thousand dollars.

5. Expect the first price you are given to be substantially higher than what you can buy the car for. Salespeople and sales managers are trained to "start high because you can always come down."

Don't be afraid to offer substantially less than the initial asking price. You should look at it just like the salesperson does, but in reverse—start low because you can always go higher.

If the salesman accepts your first offer, you probably offered too much. In fact, shrewd car salespeople are trained to always ask for more money, even if the offer is a good one. This is because they don't want to scare off the customer by telegraphing to the customer that he "left some money on the table."

6. If the salesperson asks you for a deposit before he or she will begin negotiating, ask whether the deposit is refundable.

A nonrefundable deposit must be disclosed in writing on the receipt in many states. Should that be printed on your receipt, insist that it be waived in writing on your buyer's order. If the dealer will not agree to this, be forewarned that he may be able to keep your deposit if you decide not to buy the car.

7. Be prepared for a lot of "back and forth" when the salesman takes your offer back to the manager. When you get close to finding a mutually acceptable price, the manager himself will often come to talk to you.

8. Don't be intimidated. Stick to your guns even when you are told it is "positively, absolutely the lowest price." Even if you think you do have the lowest price, a great strategy is to get up, walk out of the showroom

and get into your car to drive away. This will often precipitate an even better price.

When you try this, the worst-case scenario is that you really do drive home. But chances are that you can always return and buy the car the next day for the last price quoted to you.

The salesman or sales manager may tell you that you have to buy today, but nine times out of 10 that is a bluff. The only exception is when there are factory rebates and incentives expiring.

9. The last day of the month really is a good time to buy a car. The salesman's bonus money is maximized, the factory incentives are in effect, the managers are desperate to make their quotas and it is the one time of the month when the buyer has the best edge in negotiation.

Caveat emptor—let the buyer beware—could have been written specifically for what you can expect when you walk into a car dealership to negotiate the best price. You are up against experts who negotiate for a living. But if you follow my advice, you should be able to hold your own and maybe even get a great deal.

Chapter 18

Always Get an Out-the-Door Price

Many states have laws regulating and capping "fees" added onto the prices car dealers quote you. Unfortunately, not all states—including Florida, where I have my business—cap these fees.

Since state laws regarding this may vary, I am using Florida as an example, as it is what I know the best. You can be sure, though, that in most other states that don't regulate or limit these fees, what the law requires and the practices that take place are likely to be very similar to what I'm outlining here.

In Florida, state law requires only that dealers disclose on the buyer's order that this additional charge is not a local, state or federal fee, but is actually just profit to the dealer.

Almost every car dealership in Florida has this extra profit printed on its buyer's order, under an assortment of labels such as dealer fee, doc fee and dealer prep.

You aren't likely to see it on the car's price sticker and you will probably not hear any verbal disclosure by the salesperson or manager, unless you ask. If you ask, you will be told that "all other dealers charge this"—and this is almost true, although I, and a few others, don't.

Some attorneys advise that when a dealer has this additional profit printed on his buyer's order, he should not delete it for some customers and charge it to others. He can safely eliminate this extra profit, and avoid the charge of practicing price discrimination by reducing the selling price of the car in this amount, but still keeping the dealer fee amount printed on the buyer's order.

It is rarely done, because dealers do not pay their salesmen or managers a commission on the dealer fee. If you demand the price be reduced to compensate for the dealer fee, it cuts the salesman's commission.

In Florida, dealer fees range from $500 to more than $1,000 and a typical salesman's commission is 25 percent, so the salesman could lose anywhere from $125 to $250 plus.

Some states require that any dealer fees be included in the price of an advertised car. However, dealers advertising on the Internet and in direct mail often ignore this, because it is below the radar screen of the Attorney General's Office. In newspaper, TV and radio ads, one car may be advertised at a low price with a seemingly innocuous designation such as No. 1234B (the stock number of the car). That is all there is to tell the unsuspecting buyer that only one car is available at this price.

My advice is not to pay much attention to advertised car prices. Do your shopping on the Internet or by telephone. Insist on an "out-the-door" price including everything except sales tax and the cost of the license tag.

If buying a new car, get several out-the-door prices quoted on the exact same year, make, model and accessorized car. Two very good, free websites to get information on dealer costs and fair retail prices are www.kbb.com and www.edmunds.com. *Consumer Reports* magazine is also an excellent source of product and pricing information but there may be a fee for using its website.

Chapter 19

What's the True Price
of that New Car?

It is almost impossible for you to determine the true cost of a new car. This might sound crazy, but many dealers actually don't know the true cost of their cars. The manufacturers and distributors invoice their dealers for an amount that is almost always several hundred more than the true cost of the car shipped.

It's fair to say that in virtually every case, the invoice for a new car is much higher than the true cost. By true cost, I am referring to cost as defined by GAAP, generally accepted accounting principles.

This chapter will give you an idea of the added charges, dealer discounts and reimbursements, and incentives to both dealers and customers that can affect the price of a car—all of which make it difficult to get a handle on how much it will actually cost you.

For example, you probably have read about "holdback," which is covered in the chapter Holdback is Holdup for Consumers. That is an amount of money added to the invoice of a car, ranging from 1 percent to 3 percent of the MSRP, which is returned to the dealer after he has paid the invoice.

Some manufacturers also include the cost of regional advertising in the invoice, which offsets the dealer's advertising costs.

Another fairly common charge included in invoices is "floor plan assistance." This goes to offset the dealer's cost of financing the new cars in his inventory.

Another is "PDI," a pre-delivery expense that reimburses dealers for preparing the car for delivery to you.

I could name several more, depending on the manufacturer or distributor. Some of these monies returned to the dealer are not shown as profit on his financial statement and some are. Technically, a dealer could say the cost he showed you reflected all of the profit (by definition of his financial statement), but the fact would remain that more money would come back to him after he sold you the car.

To me, that's called profit.

Besides holdbacks and reimbursements for expenses, you must contend with customer and dealer incentives when trying to figure out the cost of that new car. You will probably be aware of the customer incentives, such as rebates or low financing rates, but not the dealer incentives, which can be discounts off the cost to dealers from the manufacturers.

Most dealers prefer and lobby manufacturers for dealer—rather than customer—incentives, just for that reason. Also, performance incentives are paid to dealers for selling a certain number of cars during a given time frame. These usually expire at the end of a month and are one reason why it really is smart to buy a new car on the last day of the month.

Last but not least, remember the dealer fee, dealer prep fee, doc fee or dealer inspection fee, etc., that is added to the price you were quoted by the salesperson. It is printed on the buyer's order and lumped into the real fees, such as sales tax and tag and registration fees.

Most dealers in Florida and elsewhere charge a dealer's fee, which ranges from $500 to more than $1,000. If you are making your buying decision on your perceived cost of the car, this can come to over $1,000 in additional profit to the dealer.

So you can see why it is virtually impossible to precisely know the cost of the new car you contemplate buying. Most often the salesman and sales manager are not completely versed on the cost either.

Checking the cost on a good Internet site, such as www.kbb.com or www.edmunds.com is about the best you can do. *Consumer Reports* is another good source. One reason Internet sites don't always have the real invoice price, however, is that different car distributors invoice their dealers at different prices.

Do not make a decision to buy a car because the dealer has agreed to sell it to you for "X dollars above his cost/invoice." This statement is virtually meaningless.

As I have advised you in other chapters, you can only be assured of getting the best price by shopping several dealers for the exact same car and getting an "out-the-door" price plus tax and tag only.

Chapter 20

What to Do if You are Treated Badly by a Car Dealer

The sales or service experience with your car dealer should go well. But sometimes it doesn't. Now what? The advice I give applies to all business transactions, not just those with car dealerships.

Your first step should be to communicate your complaint as soon as possible to the general manager (GM) or, preferably, the owner. Be sure that you are talking to the real owner or the real general manger. A GM is over all employees in the entire company. A "general sales manager" is not a general manager.

If you can't reach the owner—many car dealerships are either publicly owned or owned by absentee owners—ask to see the general manager. Often, the owner and/or general manager are not aware of everything that goes on with all their customers and employees.

They might have a new employee who should not have been hired or who received inadequate training. Or they may simply have a rotten apple that should not be working there.

The ease and speed with which you can meet and speak to a general manager or an owner is a pretty good measure of the integrity of the company as a whole. If the owner or general manager cares enough about his or her customers to allow total access, it is probably a very good place to do business. In fact, if possible, it is a good idea to find this out before you begin to do business.

If you cannot reach the owner or general manager, contact the manufacturer that franchises the dealership. Car dealers have a contract with the manufacturer called a franchise agreement. This contractual agreement requires that they treat their customers with courtesy, efficiency and integrity.

Most manufacturers have a customer hot line that allows you to call and register a complaint directly. The owner or general manager of the dealership will be made aware of your complaint. As you might guess, manufacturers have quite of bit of clout with their dealers. If dealers don't live up to their side of the contract, their franchise could be canceled or not renewed.

The third step I recommend, if Nos. 1 and 2 don't work, is to contact a consumer agency such as the Better Business Bureau or the county office of consumer affairs. These agencies will send your complaint to the dealership and request a written reply. No car dealership or business wants an unanswered complaint in the file of a governmental or private consumer agency.

The fourth step is to call your state's department of motor vehicles and/or its attorney general's office. These are extreme steps to be used for serious, even illegal, activities. The motor vehicles department will usually have the power to suspend or cancel dealers' motor vehicle retail license, putting them out of business.

The attorney general's office can file criminal charges. Dealers could be assessed large fines, or even receive jail terms, if found guilty of those charges.

Your last resort is to contact an attorney. I list this last, because hiring an attorney just about eliminates the possibility that you can quickly, amicably and inexpensively resolve your differences with the car dealer.

Be very careful which attorney you choose. Try to choose one who is primarily interested in helping you and not in generating large fees.

Under the Florida Deceptive and Unfair Trade Practices Act and similar laws in some other states, an attorney is entitled to fees and costs from the defendant in a lawsuit if he or she wins.

These fees can be much larger than the amount of your claim, motivating an unethical attorney to spend more time than needed dragging out a case to generate more fees than necessary.

This can be very dangerous for you in another way as well, because the car dealer's attorney's fees run roughly parallel to your lawyer's and you can be held liable for those if you lose the case—even if you pay nothing to your own attorney.

I hope you will never have to resort to hiring a lawyer but in trying steps one, two, three and even four, try to present your complaint as concisely and as courteously as possible.

You have every right to be angry when you are taken advantage of, but try to let your anger subside before you speak to or write to someone about your problem. We all react negatively to people who are profane, raise their voice or who are sarcastic. Your goal of communicating and resolving your complaint is best reached by communicating clearly, politely and concisely.

Chapter 21

Get it in Writing!

Many people who've read my columns call me for advice and also tell me horror stories about their dealings with unethical car dealers. Of course, it would have been much better had these readers called me before they bought the car. I have written approximately 300 columns on buying and maintaining cars for a local newspaper, and given advice on a variety of subjects to help make your car-buying or servicing experience better, safer and more pleasant.

There is one piece of advice, which, if strictly followed, would eliminate more than 90 percent of the problems car buyers have with car dealers. That advice is: Always insist that all promises and commitments made by the car salesperson or sales manager are put in writing.

The written commitments should be signed by the salesperson/manager and you should retain a copy. These are just some examples of verbal promises made by salespeople and sales managers that were not kept:

- Sign the contract, drive the car home and if you change your mind within three days you can bring the car back and we will refund all of your money. When the customer brought the car back, the salesman claimed he never said any such thing.

- After a customer signed a 36-month lease, the saleswoman assured this customer that, if she got tired of this car in less than 36 months, she could bring it back anytime. Of course, the leasing company — a company or institution that actually owns a leased car — didn't agree with the saleswoman on this.

- A customer was promised that she would be able to get free loaner cars anytime she brought her car in for service. The service department didn't know anything about this. It didn't offer free loaners.

- The business manager, also known as the F&I manager, told the customer that the warranty/extended service contract he was selling her covered 100 percent of anything that went wrong with her car. When she came in for a brake job, the service manager showed her the fine print in the warranty contract that said maintenance items were not covered.

- A salesman told the customer not to trade her car in on the new car because she owed way more on her current car than it was worth. He told her to just let the bank take the old car back and, because she was making the payments on time on her new car, it wouldn't harm her credit rating. I don't think this requires any explanation.

- Customers are promised that they can bring their cars back after they buy them and have CD players, leather, running boards and floor mats and other accessories installed as part of the deal. When they come back, none of the managers knows about this and the salesman can't be found or doesn't "remember."

I could list dozens more of these anecdotes.

You have very little chance when it's your word against the salesperson's or sales manager's. You have even less of a chance if it's two against one. Do not be timid about asking that everything you are promised be put into writing.

If the salesman objects to this or hesitates, you have to ask yourself why. Another reason for having all promises committed to writing is that the salesman or sales manager may not work at that dealership when you come back to collect on his promise. He may have actually been sincere, but now he's gone. Will his replacement believe you?

It's a good idea to carry a note pad with you when you are negotiating to buy a car. Also, as I suggested in the chapter Never Go Car Shopping Alone, be sure to have an ally with you. She can take notes while you are negotiating and also, if you do forget to commit a promise to writing, your credibility is enhanced when it's two against one instead of he said/she said.

When you are signing the final documents, you should have your complete set of notes detailing promises, assurances and commitments made by the salesman, and make sure that all of these are included in the documents before you sign them.

Then, all you have to do is have these signed by both parties and be sure that you have a copy of them.

Section Three

F&I
(Finance and Insurance)

Chapter 22

Shop Financing, Interest Rate and Trade-In When Buying a New Car

If you have read my earlier chapters, you know how important it is to get several competitive prices from different car dealers on the car you are buying. Equally important is to get at least three prices/bids on your financing and also on the true value of your trade-in.

The absolute worst thing you can do is to tell the dealer, "All I care about is keeping my payments under X dollars per month," and not know what interest rate, terms or products are included in the payments.

Part of the profit a dealer makes on his cars is called "F&I income" (finance and insurance) and ranges from $500 to as much as $2,000 or more per car sold. You can do your homework and buy your car at a very good price. But without shopping your financing, you could end up paying the dealer thousands of dollars in finance profits.

Credit unions are often the best source of funds for buying a car. Because they get special tax breaks from the government not available to banks, they usually have the lowest finance rates. Even if you don't belong to a credit union now, there are several you can join for a nominal fee.

You should also get a financing quote from the bank you do business with. In addition, give the dealer you are buying from an opportunity to beat the rates you were quoted. Sometimes he can.

When you are taking delivery of your car, you will be asked to consider buying products such as extended warranties, maintenance plans, road-hazard insurance, GAP insurance, roadside assistance, credit life insurance, etc.

My suggestion is that you do not make a snap decision on these products at the last minute. You should get complete information on each product beforehand and determine if it has value for you. You may already have similar or the same coverage for some insurance products in policies you already own. With extended warranties and maintenance, be sure you understand what is covered and what is not covered and what the deductibles are.

As I mentioned earlier, you should get at least three bids on the value of your trade-in, as well. You can get some pretty good guidance from *Kelley Blue Book* (www.kbb.com) and from www.edmunds.com.

Make an appointment to show your trade-in to the used-car manager at a dealer who is franchised to sell the make you own. A Chevrolet dealer will be likely to pay you more for a Chevrolet trade-in than a Ford dealer would. That's because people generally will shop for a used Chevy from a Chevrolet dealer.

Get one or two more bids from other dealers of the same make. If you are near a CarMax store, you should take your car there, too. CarMax regularly buys used cars for its inventory.

The price you will be quoted is referred to as the ACV, which stands for actual cash value. This is the wholesale value of your trade-in.

Don't confuse the ACV with the trade-in allowance the dealer you are buying from gives you. The trade-in allowance includes part of the markup on the vehicle you are purchasing. You have probably read ads saying, "Minimum $4,000 allowance on all trades." It's not hard to offer thousands more on a trade-in than its ACV when you mark up the new car by several thousand dollars more.

Be sure you explain that you want to compare the ACV of your trade-in. Tell the dealer you want the markup on the price of the car you are buying discounted, not added on to the ACV of your trade.

Unless you reside in one of the few remaining states with no sales tax, however, you could lose the advantage of deducting the trade-in from the price your sales tax is calculated on – if you sell it to a third party. In other words, you could lose your tax advantage if you don't trade in your old car to the dealer from whom you're buying your new car,

At 6 percent, for example, you could pay an extra $600 in sales tax for a trade-in with a $10,000 ACV.

With competitive bids on the car you are buying, the interest rate on your financing and your trade-in ACV, you are sure to minimize the total cost of that new or used car.

Chapter 23

Buying a Car When You Have a Credit Problem

There are fewer things more sensitive or embarrassing than having to share your personal credit problems with a stranger.

Having credit problems can also put many buyers in a weakened and defensive position when buying a car. Many people with bad or too little credit feel like the car dealer is somehow doing them a favor by selling them a car and getting them financed.

Make no mistake about it. A car dealer is probably making more money selling a person with bad credit a car than one with good credit.

If you have a credit problem, go about buying a car with the same care and due diligence as if you had the very best credit. Shop and compare your financing, your interest rate and your trade-in allowance. Get at least three quotes on each of these.

Lenders who specialize in lending to those with bad credit are known as "special-finance" lenders. Many of these lenders charge the dealer a large upfront fee, as much as $2,500.

Legally, the dealer is not supposed to add this fee to the price of the car you buy, but in the real world, the price of the car is usually higher because of this fee.

In addition to an upfront fee, the interest rates are very high from special-finance lenders. Because of the much higher risk and the amounts of repossession losses, more must be made on each transaction.

Don't automatically accept a dealer's opinion that you must finance through such a lender. There are conventional banks that loan to people with bad credit. Their interest rates are likely to be lower and they don't charge large upfront fees.

There is much fraud in special-finance lending. Credit applications can be falsified to show more time on the job, higher incomes, etc. W-2 forms and check stubs are counterfeited. Buyers' orders show accessories and equipment that do not really exist on the car.

Held checks or promissory notes are misrepresented as cash down payments. Co-signers' signatures are forged. Confederates pose as employers, answering phones set up to verify employment.

These falsifications are performed by finance managers, salesmen, brokers for special-finance lenders—who are paid on commission—and even the customers themselves.

If you sign a credit application, be sure that you know that all the information on that application is accurate. Be sure you understand and agree to all parts of the transaction, including down payments, accessories on the car, etc. Never be a party to falsifying information to a lender to obtain a loan. This is a criminal offense.

Advertisements aimed at people with bad credit usually exaggerate with claims such as, "We finance everyone," "Wanted, good people with bad credit," "No credit, no problem" and, my favorite, "No credit application refused" (it doesn't say your loan won't be refused, just your application).

My advice is to ignore these kinds of ads and these kinds of dealers. Their strategy is to take advantage of people with bad credit who they believe will buy any car, pay any amount of interest and at any profit to dealers as long as the dealer can get them a loan.

It is a common practice to encourage car buyers to drive the car home immediately upon signing all of the papers. In some states such as New York, however, this is not permitted until the car has been registered with the state in the new owner's name. The reason for this immediate delivery—usually referred to as spot delivery—is to discourage and possibly even prevent the buyer from changing his or her mind.

Taking possession of the car is a legal consideration making the purchase more binding. I recommend that you not rush the purchase or the delivery—you want to make sure the car is exactly the way you want it.

But more importantly, I mention the risk of the spot delivery when buying a car with bad credit, because it can be especially harmful to someone whose credit is denied after the car has been delivered.

You will most likely be required to sign a "rescission agreement" before you drive the car home. This is a legal document that requires you to return the car if your credit is denied. You will probably be told that your credit will be approved, but sometimes the dealer is wrong.

The rescission agreement will have a charge for any time and mileage that you have put on the car. These charges are usually very high, from 15 to 25 cents per mile, plus $50 per day and higher.

It can take weeks for a special-finance lender to rule on a credit application. If your credit is denied, you could owe the dealer thousands of dollars that even your down payment might not cover.

As frightening as all of the above may sound, the one single thing you can do to prevent bad things from happening when you purchase a car is to choose your car dealer very carefully.

How long has he been in business? What is his track record with the Better Business Bureau, the county office for consumer affairs and your state attorney general's office?

Ask friends, neighbors or relatives who have dealt with this car dealer what their experiences have been like. Choosing a good dealer with integrity will resolve 95 percent of all your concerns.

Chapter 24

Don't Be Spotted, Puppy-Dogged or Yo-Yoed

One of the most common unethical (and some say illegal) sales practices of car dealers is the infamous "spot delivery." If you've ever bought a car, there's a pretty good chance you have been "spotted," "puppy-dogged" and/or "yo-yoed."

Upwards of 60 percent of all car sales here in Florida are spotted. A "spot" is short for spot delivery, which is literally translated into delivering your new or used car purchase immediately—that is, "on the spot."

The spot occurs as soon as you've picked out your car and signed all the papers. The car dealer has a lot of reasons to do this. The biggest reason is so you won't change your mind about buying that car.

Legally, a contract is more binding when the seller and buyer have exchanged "consideration." Your consideration to the dealer was paying him for the car, which includes down payments, and/or a trade-in and a contract promising to make monthly payments. The dealer's consideration to you is the car, which becomes consummated when you drive it home.

Another reason why you won't change your mind is that you will take the car home, park it in your driveway and tell your neighbors, friends and relatives that you just bought a new car.

You might also brag about the fact that you have good credit, got a great price, a low interest rate and a low down payment. Everybody will envy you because you can afford that new car, were so smart to negotiate such a good price, and had such good credit that you got the lowest interest rate and down payment.

When you fall into this trap, you've just been puppy-dogged. Have you ever bought a puppy for your kids and brought it home from the pet store? Your kids play with the new puppy and take it over to their friends' houses to brag and tell them what great parents they have. What are the odds that you're going to snatch that puppy out of your child's arms and take it back to the pet store, even if it poops on your carpet?

As if all that isn't enough, the dealer has another reason to spot deliver your car.

If you traded in your old car, you can't compare the price you paid for your new car elsewhere because you no longer have your trade-in.

Dealers have a vernacular for this, too. It's called "de-horsing." In fact, dealers will often de-horse a prospect before he picks out a new car and/or signs the papers. They will give him a demo to drive home just so that they can keep him from comparing the trade-in allowance on his old car.

In fact, the delivery consideration and the "puppy dog" are such strong tools to keep you from bringing the car back that the dealer needs an ace in the hole just in case he wants you to bring the car back.

This could be because he wants or needs you to pay more for the car, pay a higher interest rate or down payment, or have a co-signer on the installment sales contract.

The dealer's ace in the hole is another contract known as the "yo-yo," or rescission agreement. This piece of paper, which you might not even remember signing, says that you have to bring your new car back if the dealer cannot find a lender who will approve your credit, down payment, interest rate and/or amount financed.

A yo-yo goes out and back and, of course, rescission means the contract is canceled. The yo-yo agreement says that if you refuse to bring the car back, the dealer can repossess the car and charge you a high fee for its usage until you do bring it back, like 25 cents a mile and $50 a day, plus the costs of recovery.

If the dealer did not have this agreement signed, you could keep the car and make your monthly payments to the dealer at the terms and conditions you originally signed. Dealers won't do this because they don't get all of their money up front like they do when they sell the finance contract to the bank. They also don't like it because they assume the credit risk if the buyer defaults.

An interesting question to ponder is whether a dealer knew in advance that he could not find a lender who would finance your car with such a low down payment, such a low interest rate, for that little number of months. Why would he do such a terrible thing?

Well, he might think that you will fall in love with that car so deeply that you will agree to pay him more profit in terms of higher interest and down payment.

He might know that you won't want to suffer the embarrassment of telling your family, friends and neighbors that your credit isn't as good as you told them it was and you really weren't so smart about your negotiations.

There's even a good argument to be made for the fact that the spot delivery is illegal and perhaps even criminal, because it's a violation of the federal Truth in Lending Act (TILA).

Without getting too technical, the signing of the yo-yo agreement also violates TILA because it means that the dealer is not the actual creditor. The finance contract you and he signed is almost meaningless and used only to take you out of the market. The only meaning is that you may have the option of signing a new contract, but this one might be for more money down, a higher interest rate and/or longer terms.

If you're interested in the legal specifics of why the spot delivery and yo-yo agreement are illegal and possibly criminal, visit this website: http://www.earlstewart.com/pdf/spot.pdf.

This is a legal memo written by an attorney, Raymond Ingalsbe, an expert on car dealers' illegal practices. He has practiced law in Palm Beach County, Fla., for more than 40 years and sues only car dealers.

He even helps train other lawyers how to sue car dealers. In fact, he sued me several times before I cleaned up my act and entered my phase as a "recovering car dealer."

The bottom line is that you should not allow yourself to be spot delivered. Whether it's illegal or not, it's certainly not a smart move for the buyer. You wouldn't move into a new home before the bank approved your mortgage would you?

When you drive that new or used car home, be sure that your credit has been approved by the lender for all terms and conditions, such as interest rate, number of months you pay, down payment and who signed the contract—for example, is a co-signer required?

If that means waiting a few days, that's good, too, because it allows you time to think over a very important decision.

Buying a new car is the second-largest purchase most people make in their lives and should never be rushed.

Chapter 25

Understanding Your New Car Warranty

A "bumper-to-bumper" warranty sounds like it means that everything is covered. Unfortunately, this is not the case. For example, tires are not covered by the car manufacturer, but under a separate warranty by the tire manufacturer. It can be tedious, but the only way to completely understand your new-car warranty is to actually read it. All warranties now are required to use the word limited unless there are absolutely zero exclusions and this, to the best of my knowledge, is never the case.

Some of the most common items that are mistakenly believed to be included in warranties are tires, rental-car coverage, maintenance, and paint faded or damaged by various kinds of air contaminants.

I don't know why all car manufacturers choose to exclude tires from their bumper-to-bumper warranties. After all, they choose the tire manufacturer just like they choose the manufacturers of other components on your car that they don't manufacture themselves, such as the sound systems.

If all went well with the car-buying experience, there's a good chance the owner will have also established a positive relationship with the service department of the dealership where she bought her car. It would be far more customer-friendly for the manufacturer to allow her dealer to handle warranty claims on tires.

My suggestion is to ask your dealer's service adviser or service manager to broker (that is, handle) the warranty claim on your tires on your behalf.

The dealership is more likely to have an established relationship with a tire store and it can be your advocate.

New-car warranties virtually never provide for a free rental car unless the vehicle must be tied up overnight for repairs. All too often, a car salesman will promise you a "free loaner" anytime your car is in for service. Verify this with the service department before you rely upon it.

There are extended service contracts, which you can buy in addition to your new-car warranty that will provide rental-car coverage.

A new-car warranty only covers repairs, not maintenance items. A very common request is that a front-end alignment be performed under warranty. Your alignment should have been checked before your car was delivered, but you should insist that it is done just before you take delivery.

Ask to be shown the computer printout showing the alignment measurements. Don't ever accept a "visual or driving check." A proper alignment check can only be done on a modern alignment machine.

If your car goes out of alignment after delivery, it is usually considered owner's maintenance but is sometimes covered by warranty for a period of time. Toyota, for example, currently covers one alignment under warranty for the first year after purchase.

Brakes are another item often misunderstood as being covered under warranty. Brake wear is almost always a maintenance item. Only a mechanical defect in your brakes is covered under warranty.

Faded or pitted paint can be from defective or improperly applied paint or from external causes like industrial fallout or foreign substances sprayed in the air (crop dusters or insect control airplanes). Of course a good argument can be made that paint should have resistance to a certain amount of air pollution.

This type of claim may require the inspection by a factory representative to determine the cause. From my experience, certain colors of paint seem to have more problems than others.

Red and white come to mind. Ask the factory service representative if he or she has experienced problems with your particular color. Stand your ground if you feel that the factory should make good for faded or pitted paint.

Get a second opinion from your insurance adjustor. You might even have an insurance claim. If you have your car washed and waxed regularly and keep it garaged, it is highly unlikely that you will ever have a paint problem.

The manufacturer's representative can authorize repairs to your car when it is out of warranty. This is called "goodwill," which is covered more extensively elsewhere in the book in the section on Service.

Often the service manager of the dealership can also authorize good-will repairs. This is a subjective ruling and depends on how close to being under factory warranty the car is, how regularly you maintained the vehicle according to factory recommendations, how many cars of this make you have bought, and how you present your request.

A car that is out of warranty by just a few miles or weeks can usually be covered under goodwill. If you maintained your vehicle regularly with your dealer and have bought several cars from this dealer, the more likely you will be to receive goodwill repairs on a car further out of warranty. Presenting your case in a positive, courteous manner helps a lot.

Service managers and factory representatives have high-pressure jobs and are often confronted by loud, rude, demanding customers. Your claim may be absolutely legitimate, but rudeness will get you nowhere. Courtesy enhances your chances of success.

Some manufacturers offer longer warranties than others. The amount of time and number of miles that a vehicle is covered is important, but it is the quality of the vehicle that is more important.

Sometimes manufacturers will increase their warranty coverage to sell more cars because the quality of their cars is in question. Quality trumps length of warranty and I would always advise buying the higher-quality car rather than the one with the longest warranty.

Chapter 26

Should You Buy an Extended Warranty?

"Should I buy an extended warranty on my new or used car?" is one of the most common questions I get asked. Extended warranties are also referred to as extended service contracts.

This is how I answer this frequent question: An extended warranty is simply a warranty that kicks in after the manufacturer's warranty expires. But extended warranties are never as comprehensive as the manufacturer's.

A manufacturer's warranty on a new car is about as close to a bumper-to-bumper warranty as you can get, except that the tire manufacturer covers the tires. There are other exclusions as well, particularly for maintenance and "wear-and-tear" items.

An extended warranty is also far from a complete bumper-to-bumper warranty, but many car salesmen and finance managers will say their extended warranty is bumper-to-bumper. This is not true.

This is sometimes referred to as the "protected payment program." This is not true either and is a violation of the Truth in Lending Act (TILA), a federal offense.

When the dealer (or anyone else) tries to sell you an extended warranty, he will focus on all of the things that the warranty covers but typically avoids telling you those items the warranty doesn't cover.

My first piece of advice is to determine exactly what is not covered by this warranty. Today's automobile contains more computer hardware and software than it took to put the first man on the moon. Computer modules are very expensive to replace and are usually not covered by extended warranties.

Navigation systems are very expensive and usually not covered. Sometimes some or all of the air-conditioning system is not covered and this is another very expensive item to repair and replace.

The more expensive a part of your car is to fix or replace, the less likely it is to be covered by the extended warranty.

All extended warranties cover the power train, which consists of the engine lower block, drive shaft and rear axle. It essentially covers the parts lubricated by your engine oil.

These components rarely fail. If they do fail, it's caused by lack of maintenance or abuse, in which case the warranty won't cover the repairs anyway.

You'll see a lot of dealers advertising a "free lifetime warranty" with every car they sell. These are power-train warranties and they are free because they are virtually worthless.

If you decide to buy an extended warranty, be sure you know the company that stands behind the warranty. Check out the company's financial stability. It's not uncommon for warranty companies to go broke and then you're stuck with a worthless warranty.

Many manufacturers offer extended warranties and these are generally safer bets than independent companies. If the dealer is selling his own warranty, make sure that he is financially strong and that you don't have to bring your car back to that particular dealer anytime you have a repair covered by the warranty. You should have the right to have your car repaired by any service department in North America that sells your brand of car.

If you ever receive a solicitation to buy an extended warranty in the mail, by email or by telephone, ignore it. Ninety-nine percent of these are scams. The warranties are overpriced and cover virtually nothing that might need repairs—again, usually just a power-train warranty.

The companies offering them are likely to be gone when you try to make a claim. These companies (many seem to be based in Las Vegas) buy mailing and email lists from the various states' departments of motor vehicles. They know your name, address, when you bought your car and the make and model from this data.

So they also know when your car will be out of the manufacturer's warranty by how long you've owned it. A lot of these solicitations appear to be coming from the manufacturer, but manufacturers never solicit their owners for extended warranties. The envelope and letters are made to look very official and threatening, giving you only a few days to act before it's too late.

PHOTOGRAPHS

E. D. STEWARD

New Sales Manager for the Williams Motor Sales Company

Williams motor sales company, local dealers in Dodge Bros' motor cars, has announced the appointment of a new sales manager. "We feel singularly fortunate," said Mr Williams, president of the local concern, in having secured the services of Mr Stewart for this important position. Stewart came direct from Dodge Bros' Detroit offices to take charge of our sales department, and I know he will become very popular with our patrons. He is unusually well informed on the policies and product of the great Detroit organization. Mr Stewart is a graduate of the Detroit college of law, but left that profession several years ago to enter the automobile field. During a large part of his three years with Dodge Bros at Detroit, he had thus become very familiar with eastern business conditions and methods. Mr Stewart has had wide mechanical, as well as business experience with motor cars. Previous to his association with Dodge Bros he spent a number of months as traveling service instructor for the Maxwell company. Big, efficient and good natured, Stewart will prove popular addition to the local personnel of automobile men, and we prohesy his success in the new field.

Earl Stewart Sr. featured in news article, 1917

FORM D S A 501

CAR INVOICE
CUSTOMERS COPY

~~STEWART-OBEE INC~~
~~CORTELYOU PONTIAC SALES, Inc.~~

508 So. Olive Ave.   Telephone 4647

WEST PALM BEACH, FLA.

February 17 1937

SOLD TO Annia Swan

ADDRESS 4 El Bravo Way
Palm Beach, Fla.

SALESMAN Clark

MAKE	MODEL	NEW OR USED	SERIAL NO.	MOTOR NO.	KEY NO.	DESCRIPTION	AMOUNT	
Pontiac	1937	N	6CA-44093	6-262653		2 Dr. Trg. Se	$914	00
						NEW CAR FREIGHT AND HANDLING		
						TIME PRICE DIFFERENTIAL AND INSURANCE		
							10	50
						TOTAL SALE	$930	50
						SETTLEMENT		
						CASH ON DELIVERY	795	50
						PREVIOUS DEPOSIT		
						USED CAR	135	00
						TYPE		
						SERIAL NO.		
						MOTOR NO.		
						NOTES:—		
							$930	50
						TOTAL		

THE REYNOLDS & REYNOLDS CO., DAYTON, O.

D S A 501

ALWAYS SHOW SERIAL, MOTOR AND KEY NUMBER

PRINTED IN U.S.A.

APPN. NO. 565909

MOTOR VEHICLE CERTIFICATE OF TITLE

CERT. NO. 1147609

STATE OF FLORIDA

TALLAHASSEE, FLA., Mar 10, 1937

SATISFACTORY PROOF HAVING BEEN MADE UNDER CHAPTER 9157, ACTS OF 1923, THAT TITLE TO THE MOTOR VEHICLE HEREINAFTER DESCRIBED IS VESTED IN THE OWNER NAMED BELOW. THIS OFFICIAL CERTIFICATE OF TITLE IS ISSUED FOR THE MOTOR VEHICLE DESCRIBED AS FOLLOWS:

NAME AND MAKE Pontiac   TYPE sedan Trg WHEELS 5 steel

ENGINE NUMBER 6-262653   MODEL 6CA   CYLS 6

SERIAL NO. 6CA-44093   YEAR OF MAKE 1937 OTHER DESCRIPTIVE FEATURES

TAG NO. D56041   LIENS $ None

(Kind of Liens)

NAME: Annie Swan

ADDRESS: 4 El Bravo Way
Palm Beach, Florida

Bill of sale and title to a 1937 Pontiac sold to Annie Swan, the first car ever sold by the Stewart family car business. It was repurchased from Mrs. Swan in 1961 and has been restored and now sits in the showroom of Earl Stewart Toyota.

Earl Stewart Jr., circa 1941

Stewart Pontiac dealership, established by Earl Stewart Sr. and later owned by his sons Earl Stewart Jr. and Douglas Stewart. It was a landmark business in West Palm Beach at 1928 South Dixie Highway in the Flamingo Park business district until it was sold and demolished in 1999.

Earl Stewart Sr. with a customer in 1947

Earl Stewart Sr. with an employee at Stewart Pontiac In 1947

Earl Stewart Sr. and Douglas Stewart, to the right, with the painting of Chief Pontiac, which was displayed in the Stewart Pontiac dealership for many years.

Earl Stewart Sr. with son Earl Stewart Jr. at Camp Arrowhead in Tuxedo, North Carolina

Virginia Stewart and husband Earl Stewart Sr. near their West Palm Beach home, circa 1951

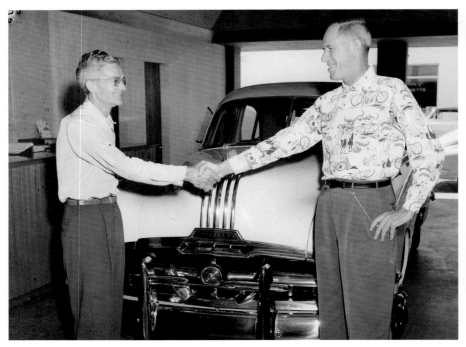

Earl Stewart Sr., right, congratulates a customer on his new Pontiac, circa 1952.

Stewart Pontiac service department, circa 1954

Earl Stewart Sr., center, and Virginia Stewart, seated in striped dress, relax at home with family friends Jack and Esther Curry, circa 1955.

Virginia Stewart and Earl Stewart Sr. pose along Flagler Drive in West Palm Beach with their children Barbara and Earl Stewart Jr., holding the family pet dachshund Junior, circa 1956.

Gloria Stewart and husband Douglas Stewart in Key Biscayne in a Pontiac
Bonneville in 1957

Earl Stewart Jr. 1958 senior
picture, Palm Beach High School

Virginia and Earl Stewart Sr. on a fishing trip, circa 1959

Stewart Pontiac dealership, featuring open-air showroom and neon signage, circa 1960

Stewart Pontiac showroom was reopened after a service department fire damaged the dealership in 1960.

A life-sized statue of Chief Pontiac getting a makeover, circa 1960. This plaster statue, which was displayed in the open-air showroom, was frequently "borrowed" by Palm Beach High School fraternity members, who would "relocate" it to the beach or atop a public building as a school prank.

Earl Stewart Sr. with Annie Swan as she traded in her 1937 Pontiac, the first car ever sold by the dealership

Service tech Dean Hamilton, Stewart Pontiac, circa 1962

Stewart Pontiac service department, circa 1962, featuring then state-of-the-art diagnostic equipment, a tradition carried on to this day at Earl Stewart Toyota.

Stewart Pontiac service department, circa 1962

Stewart Pontiac service department, circa 1963

Douglas Stewart, circa 1968

View of Carefree Theater through rubble of remodeling Stewart Pontiac, 1969

Artist rendering for remodeled Stewart Pontiac

Earl Stewart Sr., circa 1969

Earl Stewart Jr., 1971

Pontiac dealers with Earl Stewart Jr. in the back row, far right, circa 1974

Earl Stewart Sr., circa 1974

Earl Stewart Jr., Earl Stewart Sr. and Douglas Stewart in the newly remodeled Stewart Pontiac, 1969

Stewart Automotive Group grew to include Stewart Mazda, the first Mazda dealership in the southeastern United States, in 1975. The dealership was located on Olive Avenue behind Stewart Pontiac and later moved to a location on Dixie Highway at Flamingo Drive, diagonally across from Stewart Pontiac.

Earl Stewart Jr. with longtime employee James Andrews, and Douglas Stewart, at Andrews' retirement party. He was the new car detailing manager with Stewart Pontiac for thirty years, and was presented a new yellow Pontiac Phoenix from the Stewart family on his retirement.

Douglas Stewart, Stewart Toyota Service Manager Jerry Roach, Stewart Toyota Comptroller Lee Miller, Southeast Toyota District Representative Al Hendrickson Sr., Stewart Toyota Parts Manager Stan Bausinger and Kick Ludwig of Southeast Toyota receive an award from Southeast Toyota.

Douglas Stewart, far left and Earl Stewart Jr., far right, with members of the Stewart Pontiac sales and leadership team, Bob Lichty, Norm Keller, Mike Whalen, Doug Putnam, Mike Whitten, and Ron Glinten

West Palm Beach Mayor Nancy Graham joins Douglas Stewart and Earl Stewart Jr. in cutting a ribbon for the Flamingo shopping district historic exhibit at the Stewart Pontiac dealership, part of the celebration of the West Palm Beach Centennial in 1994.

Earl Stewart Toyota Comptroller Janet Goetz at a Halloween party in the 1980s. Janet has worked at the Stewart family dealerships since 1964 and is one of its most valued employees.

Demolition of Stewart Pontiac, 1999 *Photo by Richard Graulich*

Earl Stewart stands in the showroom of his Toyota dealership in Lake Park, Florida. This photo appeared in the *Palm Beach Post* as part of a story on the dealership announcing Earl Stewart's Internet blog "Earl Stewart on Cars." *Photo by Palm Beach Post*

The company yacht, Kaizen, which means continual improvement in Japanese. Earl Stewart regularly allows employee groups to use the vessel for fishing or sightseeing cruises.

Earl Stewart in the service bay at Earl Stewart Toyota dealership. *Photo by Automotive News*

Earl Stewart and his wife Nancy Stewart host a weekly radio call in show on Seaview Radio every Saturday from 9–10 a.m. It is the most popular local radio show in that time slot. The No Dealer Fee sign behind him refers to Earl Stewart's statewide campaign to eliminate or at least limit dealer fees charged to customers. *Photo © 2008 Mike Hamel/Automotive News*

Earl Stewart established his Toyota dealership in Lake Park in 1974. The original building was demolished in 2005 to make way for a new state-of-the-art dealership. It is now one of the top sales volume dealerships in the nation with one of the highest customer service satisfaction ratings in the Southeast among Toyota dealerships.

The newly remodeled Earl Stewart Toyota dealership, completed in January 2005

Stewart Toyota Hybrid-Certified Master Diagnostic Technician Rick Kearney drove a modified Toyota Prius hybrid vehicle from North Palm Beach, Florida, to Washington, D.C., on one tank of gas, beginning June 1, 2009. The trip drew public interest and extensive media coverage at every stop along the 1,200-mile trip.

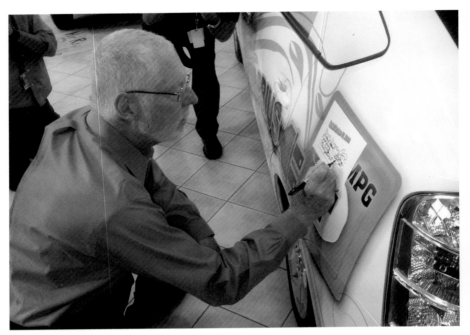

Earl Stewart and local dignitaries signed the sealed gas tank of the "Incredible Electric Green Machine" Prius prior to its record-breaking trip.

Earl Stewart gives Rick Kearney a bear hug for good luck before the Electric Green Machine trip in 2009.

The Incredible Electric Green Machine arrives at the U.S. Capitol using less than one tank of gas. On hand to congratulate driver Rick Kearney are publicist Margie Yansura, Earl Stewart, the likeness of President Obama, and Gerald Juliano.

Earl Stewart with his sons Jason, Stu and Josh, all of whom are in managerial positions in the dealership, extending the Stewart Automotive business into its third generation. *2009 photo by David Kadlubowski for Toyota Today*

The Stewart family: Nancy and Earl, with his sons Josh, Stu and Jason. *2009 photo by David Kadlubowski for Toyota Today*

Josh Stewart works with Martin Stevens at Earl Stewart Toyota on Monday, Sept. 21, 2009. *2009 photo by David Kadlubowski for Toyota Today*

Josh, Stu and Jason Stewart, sons of Earl Stewart and managers at Earl Stewart Toyota, September 21, 2009. *2009 photo by David Kadlubowski for Toyota Today*

The Stewart family celebrates with Earl Stewart Toyota employees as the dealership becomes the top volume Toyota dealership on the southeast coast of Florida.

Earl Stewart, right, is joined by Stu Stewart in presenting a check to WPTV Channel 5 news meteorologist Steve Weagle as a donation to the American Red Cross through an on-air auction of the bike Weagle used in his annual charity bike ride for the Red Cross. This is just one example of Earl Stewart Toyota's generous support of local charities.

With the ever-present red hot line in the foreground, Earl Stewart addresses new car owners at the dealership's quarterly new owners' dinner.

Earl Stewart shows the faulty accelerator pedal on one of the recalled Toyota vehicles on January 27, 2010. This picture went viral and appeared all over the world. *Photo by Associated Press*

I still haven't answered your question about whether or not you should buy an extended warranty.

You need to be very careful about which warranty you're considering and from whom you buy it. I look at an extended warranty just like I look at an insurance policy. In fact, you're lucky if you live in Florida or another state where automotive extended warranties are regulated by the state insurance commission. The rates are approved and registered with that state.

But in many states, a dealer can charge anything he can get for an extended warranty.

You may be able to cancel an extended warranty if you haven't used it anytime in the first 60 days, however. Be sure to check this out; it should be noted on the warranty if this is the case.

My philosophy is to buy insurance on something that I either couldn't afford to fix or replace or that would put a financial hardship on me if I did.

I carry fire and flood insurance on my home based on this philosophy. I don't buy an extended warranty on my iPhone because I can afford to buy another one if mine broke.

If you think it will bring you peace of mind, however, then I suggest that you may want to consider buying an extended warranty. This varies based on the personality of each individual.

Whatever you decide, just remember that most insurance companies make lots of money. This is how Warren Buffett became one of the richest men in the world.

Insurance companies take in a lot more money in premiums than they pay out in claims. They also don't have to pay taxes on the income for a long time and can invest those tax-free funds in the interim.

When you buy an insurance policy, you're betting against the house and, in the long run, you will almost always lose.

But if you got peace of mind because you protected yourself against a loss that would have severely tapped your financial resources, it may be worth it.

Chapter 27

Beware of The Box

OK, you've just bought that new or used car and the pressure is off, right?

Wrong.

The next step for the car dealer is to get you into "The Box." You won't hear this word mentioned. It's insider car-dealer slang for the business office. This is the place where you sign all of those papers making the sale legal and final.

But in addition to that, it's also a very important profit center for car dealers. In many car dealerships it's the most profitable department. It's not uncommon for car dealers to make an additional $2,000 profit or more in The Box on each car they sell. Here's how that profit is generated:

First, and usually foremost, it is by making money on the interest they charge you. Essentially, they make money on "the spread," just like banks make money when they lend it.

For example, a car dealer will borrow money from Bank of America for 2.5 percent and lend it to you for 6.5 percent, or whatever interest rate you can be persuaded to accept.

The second way dealers earn that big profit in The Box is by selling you products that are added to the price of the car you just bought. There are many of these and some of the most common are extended service warranties, maintenance plans, road-hazard insurance, GAP insurance (Guaranteed Auto Protection, which comes into play if the car is lost or stolen while the owner is still making payments), window etch, and LoJack, a popular theft recovery device.

The way you should protect yourself on the interest rate is to have already shopped your own bank or credit union and two other lending institutions for the best interest rate you can qualify for. Never go into The Box without knowing what the best rate other banks or credit unions will allow you.

The best protection against being sold products that you don't really want or need is to completely understand each one.

Do you want or need an extended warranty on your new car? If this product costs $1,900, for example, how long are you going to keep the car and how long are you likely to be driving it when it's out of the manufacturer's warranty?

Ask the same questions of each product you are being encouraged to buy. If you are unclear on the merits of a product, do not commit. You can always go home and think about it and seek advice from friends and advisers.

If the business manager, also known as the finance and insurance (F&I) manager, tells you that you must decide before you take the car home, tell him you will not buy whatever product he's trying to sell.

Another important tactic that I recommend is to never go into The Box alone. If it's just the F&I manager and you, and there is a dispute over what was said, it's just your word against his. Also, having a friend or adviser present will usually be a deterrent to any attempted deception.

There are some kinds of deception you should be on the lookout for, such as tying the sale of a product, an extended service contract, for example, to the interest rate or eligibility to have the bank finance your car. This practice is illegal, but it happens all too often behind the closed doors of The Box.

The F&I manager may tell you that the bank "requires" you to buy the extended warranty, GAP insurance or another product in order to protect the bank's collateral. This is another lie and it's illegal for banks or car dealers to do this.

Another common form of deception is simply not to disclose the products or interest rate and have you sign the contract without reading it.

There are numerous documents to be signed after you buy a car. Buyers are often in a such state of euphoria now that they have bought the car of their dreams that they are in too much of a hurry to sign everything and drive their new car home.

The car dealer is required by law to give you a signed copy of the finance installment sales contract. Be sure you carefully read it and be sure you have a copy. If you don't get one, you may find that you signed a contract different from the one you read. Many people mistakenly believe that there is a time called a "cooling off period" during which you can cancel the contract. There is such a law in some states, but it applies only to home solicitation sales, not sales in a place of business.

Extended service warranties, GAP insurance and other insurance products are regulated in some states such as Florida, where I have my business, but not in all. Where it's available, this kind of regulation affords you some degree of protection, such as being able to cancel an insurance product as long as you did not use it. You can usually do this within 60 days for a 100 percent cancellation credit as long as you have not used the policy for repairs.

You wouldn't get the cash back and your monthly payment wouldn't go down. But the amount would be taken off the principal amount you are financing through the bank.

You can sometimes cancel insurance products after 60 days, but the cancellation wouldn't be pro-rated and you would pay a large penalty.

If you remember nothing else from this chapter, please remember this one thing: Do not hurry the process of financing your car and signing the papers. Do not let the car dealer encourage you to sign anything you don't understand. Time is on your side, because it will allow you to think and consult with others who can help you make your final decision.

I get a lot of calls from victims of The Box and the one thing they all have in common is that they let themselves be rushed into signing the documents so that they could drive their dream car home that same day.

Section Four

ABOUT USED CARS

Chapter 28

Ten Tips for Buying a Used Car

I sell new and used cars, but if I was not a car dealer and needed to buy a car, I would buy a used one instead of a new one. This is because a used car is a better value. You get more for your money because you avoid the initial rapid depreciation of a new car.

Everybody knows that a new car can depreciate several thousand dollars in the first few months of ownership. This depreciation is mainly due to the psychological and emotional desire to be the first owner of a brand-new vehicle.

What other explanation is there for a current or 1-year-old model used car, with most of the new-car warranty remaining, to sell for $2,000 or $3,000 less than a new one?

A used car can also be a better buy because it has a performance track record that can be checked out.

Buyers of a new model in its first year of introduction can find themselves performing the role of test drivers. More often than not, the first year of a new model comes with some minor—and sometimes even major—bugs.

These are problems you would want to know about if you're thinking of buying a used car manufactured the year the model was introduced.

It is sometimes possible to speak to the former owner about a used car and also to review the car's service file, research its performance on the Internet and check out *Consumer Reports*.

Of course, there is more risk in buying a car that's been used. And just a note here: I use the term "used car" in this chapter because I despise mumbo jumbo euphemisms such as "pre-owned." A used car is a used car is a used car.

Here are 10 good tips for buying a used car:

1. Never buy a used car without a CarFax report. The dealer should provide you with one at no charge because any dealer worth his salt, in order to protect himself, runs a CarFax report on every used car he takes in trade or buys.

Simply don't buy a used car from anybody who does not give you this report.

CarFax reports now have not only the information about collision damage, flood damage, previous odometer reading and title issues (all obtained from insurance records) but also the mechanical repair history, obtained from dealer records.

2. Have the car inspected by an independent mechanic. Insist on having the used car you are thinking about buying inspected by your mechanic, not one affiliated with the dealer. This should cost you no more than $150 and will be money well spent.

The mechanic should look not only for mechanical issues, but also for body and flood damage. If the mechanic finds minor things that need fixing, insist that the dealer take care of these and include it in the price he has already quoted you. If the dealer won't allow this, don't buy from him.

3. Consult *Consumer Reports* or www.kbb.com and www.edmunds. com. These sources have complete information on the safety, reliability, maintenance cost and even what a fair price is to pay for any used car. *Consumer Reports* puts out an online, quick-reference Best and Worst Used Cars list every year from the results of its annual auto survey, in which subscribers rate the reliability of more than one million cars over a number of years. This is a great guide, and don't ever buy a used car that's on the Worst List.

A certified used car is only as good as the dealer who sold it to you. All manufacturers sponsor "certified" used cars of their make because they like to sell the dealer warranties that the dealer then marks up and sells to you.

A secondary reason manufacturers do this is to enhance the resale value of their make of car. This helps them sell more new cars because of the higher trade-in value as well as the higher residual values on cars that they lease, both of which enhance their profits.

You can buy a warranty for a used car even if it's not certified, but with a certified used car it's usually included in the price (which makes the price higher).

One good thing about manufacturers' certified programs is that sometimes the manufacturer will offer lower financing rates.

Certified used cars require the dealer to inspect all critical parts of the car and fill out a checklist that is anywhere from 75 to 150 items. That's all well and good, but how carefully is this inspection being done and by whom? You should ask to see a copy of the checklist and also ask about the qualifications of the mechanic who performed and signed the inspection.

All too often, the dealer assigns the lowest mechanic on the totem pole to perform these checks. Sometimes it is questionable as to whether or not all of them have been performed.

It's a red flag if you notice a straight line drawn through all of the check boxes instead of each having been checked off individually. So make certain to be on the lookout for this when you review the inspection papers.

4. **Be cautious about a money-back guarantee or exchange-of-car guarantee.** A lot of dealers advertise that if you change your mind about the car you bought you can bring it back and exchange it for another. This is a worthless guarantee. You can be sure that they will pick which car, as well as the price they will exchange it for, and will end up making an additional profit.

CarMax has a reasonable guarantee, however, which refunds all your money within five days with the restriction that the car is returned in the same condition in which it was sold. CarMax is a good place to buy a used car.

5. **Contact the previous owner of the car, if possible.** There's a good chance that the last owner of the car may be willing to talk to you. Insist the seller provide you with the previous owner's telephone number. If there is reticence to do this on the part of the dealer who wants to sell you a used car, then insist that he call the former owner requesting permission to give out the number, or that he ask the former owner to contact you.

If the dealer sold the used car to that owner as a new or used vehicle and serviced it, also ask to see the service file.

6. **Test drive the car just as you will be driving it later.** Simply taking the car for a spin around the block with the salesman is not enough. I recommend that you drive the car in the manner and places that you would be driving it if you owned it.

Take it out on the expressway if you do a lot of higher-speed driving. You should drive the car for at least a few hours at all the same speeds and conditions on the same roads that you normally experience. Park the car, back it up and take a friend for a ride to get her opinion. You don't want to have any surprises when you bring it home for keeps.

7. **The Internet is the best place to shop for your used car.** Most dealers today display all their used car inventory right on their websites, along with the prices. These prices are pretty close to the real price you will pay. Just as they do with a new car for sale, dealers know that they won't get many responses if they overprice their used cars on the Internet.

Shopping on the Internet also gives you ample opportunity to compare the same or similar used-cars prices with lots of different dealers.

As always, call the dealer before you come in to confirm the Internet price is the out-the-door price without any fees that will be added later, including a dealer's fee.

8. **Commit all of the dealer's promises to writing.** Take notes on everything the salesman and sales manager promise you, such as, "We'll fix that CD player if you'll bring your car in next week," or, "If you ever have a problem with the car, we'll give you a free loaner when you come in for service." Make sure those notes are part of the buyer's order and be sure that a manager signs it.

9. **It's also a good idea to always shop with a friend.** Just as it is when buying a new car, in a he said/she said situation, two people trump one. (See the chapter Never Go Car Shopping Alone.)

10. **Get at least three bids on financing.** Know what your lowest interest rate is for the year, make, and model car you're buying. Get quotes from your bank or credit union and at least one other bank in addition to the rate your dealer offers you.

If you do use your dealer's financing, you must still be sure you know and understand everything that's included in your finance contract.

You will be offered products such as warranties, maintenance, road hazard insurance, GAP insurance (covers the difference between what a car is worth and the amount owed in the event of theft or a "totaled" car due to an accident), etc. It's illegal, however, for a dealer to tie your acceptance for financing or interest rate to your buying a warranty or any other product.

Chapter 29

Used Car Book Value — Nobody Knows What Your Used Car is Worth

A lot of people think that all used cars have a specific value and they can learn this by looking it up in the *Blue Book* or some other used-car wholesale book. Nothing could be further from the truth.

The wholesale books that dealers use and those that are available online to consumers have varying degrees of accuracy, but you can't rely on a book to tell you the best price at which you can sell or trade in your car. The most accurate "book" is the Manheim Market Report (MMR) because it's based on the latest wholesale auctions nationwide and is updated daily online.

The least accurate book is the NADA guide, which relies solely on surveys sent to dealers. The dealers exaggerate the wholesale value of their brand to make it easier to take in trades.

All of the wholesale books, except NADA, are based on prices of cars sold at auction. However, you must understand that those prices don't give you an accurate figure that you should expect for your trade.

A car sells at an auction for the price offered by the highest bidder if the seller chooses to accept that bid. I often don't sell my used cars to the highest bidder in a particular week because I might get a much higher price the next week.

Lots of things affect the level of prices at a car auction — the weather, holidays, bribing the auctioneer and bribing the buyers. On a cold, rainy day when few dealers show up to buy or sell cars, prices are lower, as well as shortly before and after holidays.

A car doesn't even have to go through the auction block for the owner to believe it was sold at the auction. Buyers and sellers can make a deal before it goes "through the block"—very cozy, only one bidder.

Why would they do that? Often the buyers and sellers are employed by the dealer who actually owns the car. They are "shills," if you will, there to drive up the price to an acceptable level.

The used-car manager or wholesale buyer employed by the dealer might pay $2,000 too much for a car if he can get $500 cash in his pocket from the seller. His boss, the dealer, is never the wiser.

Let me hasten to add that the Manheim auctions are very careful to police these kinds of shenanigans and never encourage them. However, as in every large organization (Manheim is the largest auto auction in the world), there can be a few rotten apples.

You may be thinking, "OK then, if the books are wrong and the auctions are wrong, then surely the car dealer must know the value of my trade-in." Wrong again.

I have a little test on used-car appraisal knowledge that I administer to my sales managers from time to time. By the way, my managers are among the most knowledgeable and competent anywhere. This isn't just my opinion, but that of all their peers in this market.

My test goes like this: Without prior notice, I randomly select a car from among the 100 or so that come into my service department each day. I ask each of my eight managers individually to appraise this car for what they think the current wholesale market value is. They keep their appraisal from the others and write it down on a piece of paper and hand it to me. I've been doing this for 30 or more years and I've never had a variance in appraisals of less than $3,000. Some have been greater than $10,000!

The reason I do this is to remind all of my managers of exactly what I'm explaining in this chapter: Nobody knows the exact value of a used car. That's important for my managers to know because under-appraising a used car can cost us a sale.

Over-appraising a used car can cost us a wholesale loss at the auto auction. Therefore, we always check and recheck our appraisals and go so far as to call other dealers.

Another good reason not to accept only one dealer's appraisal is that dealers will often knowingly undervalue your trade-in, especially if you've negotiated a very low price for your new car. The dealer vernacular for this is "stealing the trade."

Now that we've established that nobody has any idea what your trade-in is worth, what does that mean to you? It means you should stop worrying about getting an accurate appraisal because there's no such thing.

However, what you should positively insist on is getting the highest appraisal. In fact, you should hope that the guy who gave you the highest appraisal was very inaccurate and made a huge mistake that will cost his dealership a large wholesale loss at the auction.

So never accept the appraisal by the car dealer you're buying your next car from without checking out the possibility that you might get a better deal for your trade-in elsewhere.

You should get at least two other bids from dealers of the make of car you are trading in. For example, a Ford dealer will usually appraise a Ford for more than a Honda dealer because more people wanting to buy a used Ford will shop the larger selection at a Ford dealer.

Deal directly with the used-car department at these other dealerships. Tell the used-car manager that you need to sell your car for cash and that you're getting two more bids from two other dealers. If you have the time to get more than two additional bids, it's even better.

Another good place to get a bid on your used car is from CarMax, the largest retailer of used cars in the world. It buys lots of cars directly from owners even when they don't buy a car from CarMax. Its purchase prices are sometimes higher than dealers will offer you.

So, after you determine the highest bidder, if it's not the dealer from whom you're buying, give your dealer the right of last refusal. If he can match the price from his competitor, you won't have to pay sales tax on the price of your trade.

Section Five

LEASING

Chapter 30

Find Out a Car's Residual Value Before Leasing or Buying

The purchase price of your new car is only one component in the total cost of ownership. Depreciation is the largest single cost of owning.

Two different make-and-model cars can have almost identical prices, but one can easily depreciate thousands of dollars more than the other.

For example, according to the *Automotive Leasing Guide* (*ALG*), the residual value for a 2011 Honda Fit on a 36-month lease was 52 percent. The residual value for a 2011 Chevrolet Aveo5 2LT was 34 percent. The MSRP of these two cars was $16,865 for the Chevrolet Aveo5 2 LT and $16,670 for the Honda Fit, $195 less than the Aveo5.

The Aveo5's value depreciates down to $5,734 in three years. The Accord depreciates only to $8,668. Even if you were able to buy the Aveo5 for a much larger discount than the Fit, the discount would not offset the extra depreciation, which is $2,934 more than the Accord. This—plus the $195 difference between the prices of the two cars—brings the lessee's total savings to $3,129.

The *Automotive Leasing Guide* is the "bible" that virtually all car-leasing companies (banks and other institutions or companies that finance car leases) use to establish the used-car value of a car at the end of the lease. All car dealerships, leasing companies and banks that lease cars will have a copy of this book. Your car dealer should have no problem with letting you look at its *ALG* residual book.

You can also get information from *ALG's* website, www.alg.com, (consumers can get some general information there on which cars have higher residual value, but not specifics) and you can also get information on residuals and depreciation from www.kbb.com and www.Edmunds.com.

ALG has been doing this for more than 40 years and it looks at many factors before establishing a residual number for a particular year, make and model vehicle.

For example, the residuals for Chrysler and GM products plummeted when these companies entered bankruptcy. The residuals for these makes came back, although not all the way, after the companies emerged from bankruptcy.

Typically, vehicles with large discounts and cash rebates are usually the ones that depreciate the fastest.

The biggest single factor that translates into a higher residual (low depreciation) value is high quality. Historically, Asian vehicles have typically ranked highest in quality surveys. My favorite judge of vehicle quality is *Consumer Reports* and its tests for reliability.

Another important factor in establishing depreciation rates is the price of gasoline. The residual values of trucks, vans and SUVs plummeted when the price of gas hit around $4 a gallon. As you might expect, the residual values of fuel-efficient cars, especially hybrids, soared.

With gas prices being volatile, you may want to consider leasing if you want to lock in the depreciation. You can hedge the price of gasoline and let the leasing company bear the risk or reward.

At the end of the lease on a big truck, if gas prices climb higher, the resale value will plummet, but you can simply walk away from the leased vehicle and let the leasing company absorb the loss.

On the other hand, it the price of gas should drop precipitously, although that seems unlikely, the resale/residual would rise. You could then exercise your purchase option and "flip it" (sell it back) to the dealer, who would pay you the higher wholesale value.

The bottom line is, before you are going to buy or lease your next car, don't make a final decision until you have an idea what the *ALG* residual value for that specific year, make and model is.

The higher the value, the less the cost of depreciation, which translates into a higher trade-in allowance when you're ready to buy your next vehicle. Or it could translate into being able to sell it outright for more money.

Chapter 31

Avoiding Car-Leasing Booby Traps

It seems that car dealers are resorting more than ever before to advertising car leasing. This is simply because it's easier to offer a low monthly payment with a lease ad than with a purchase ad.

But accompanying this lower payment is a number of booby traps that can trip you up badly, especially if you have never leased a car before. This chapter focuses on these hidden potential problems, sometimes buried in fine print, which you probably hadn't thought about or even suspected. Here are some of the most common:

1. <u>After you've returned the leased car, you're told you owe the bank or leasing company for excess mileage and damage beyond "normal wear and tear."</u>

The danger here is that many people return their car to the dealership after the lease expires without obtaining signed, written verification of any damage that exists on the car and what mileage is on the odometer.

Returned lease cars can sit on the car dealer's lot for weeks or even months before the bank or leasing company gets around to picking them up and sending them to auction.

Anybody might be driving that lease car in the interim. It could be an employee of the dealership. A returned lease car with a full tank of gas can be a big temptation.

In many dealerships, the accounting for returned lease cars is very sloppy. A returned lease car can easily be stolen without anyone noticing.

Remember, the car does not belong to the dealership, but to the bank or other institution that financed the lease. The dealer doesn't even have insurance on this car.

In fact, the insurance may even still be in your name unless you've had it changed, something you must make sure to do as soon as possible when returning a lease.

I have heard many horror stories of customers who received bills from their leasing company weeks after returning their leased car for thousands of dollars in damage and excess mileage that they say they were not responsible for.

Your only protection is to be sure at the time you return the leased car that a representative of the dealership fills out, with you, a complete return-lease inspection form, which notes all damage, estimated cost of repair and the mileage. Be sure this is signed by the dealership representative and that you get a copy. As an extra precaution, I recommend taking pictures of your lease return car.

2. A lease ad shows a large down payment and a short term.

Most lease ads on TV or in the newspaper have a big down payment hidden in the fine print. A down payment of $4,000 is typical.

Ironically, one of the biggest reasons people lease cars is to avoid laying out more cash. Dealers like to advertise leases because a cash down payment on a lease is "leveraged" to provide more profit to the dealer than a down payment on a purchase.

A down payment on a lease has more impact on the payment because it lowers the capitalized amount, which is just a portion of the payment — the other portion being depreciation. On the other hand, a down payment on a financed purchase lowers the total amount financed.

It's leveraged on a lease because the dealer can reduce the monthly payment as low as he wants by simply raising the down payment closer to the estimated residual value at the end of the lease. The leverage increases by shortening the term because shorter leases have higher residuals.

A $4,000 down payment on a lease will reduce the monthly payment much more than on a purchase because payments on a purchase are made until the "residual" is zero and you own the car.

This makes a lease appear more attractive to customers and also makes it possible for the dealer to make more profit. Also, watch out for shorter lease terms, such as 24 months, compared to 36 or 48, which are normal.

Remember, when buying a car, your monthly payments are paying for the whole car. When leasing, you are only paying for a small part of the car — the time you use it.

A 24-month lease requires less of a down payment to lower the monthly payment than a 36-month lease or 48-month lease. You can actually lease a car for "$0 per month" if you put up a large enough down payment. The banks call this a "one-pay lease." All you are doing is making all of your lease payment up front and, to a lesser extent, this is also what you're doing when a dealer sneaks in a large lease down payment in the fine print.

3. A low-mileage allowance is set in the contract.

Be sure you know exactly how many miles are allowed in your lease contract. By restricting the number of miles you are allowed, the dealer can quote a lower monthly payment. I've seen lease ads with as low as a 7,500 annual mileage allowance and a 15 to 25 cents-per-mile penalty. Most people drive a lot more miles than this.

If you missed this in the fine print, and are a fairly typical driver who puts 15,000 miles a year on your car, you would get a nasty surprise bill from your leasing company of $5,625 at the end of a 36-month lease.

4. The lease acquisition fee and the dealer fee are still possible.

If you thought you were going to avoid the infamous "license to steal," the dealer fee, by leasing your car, you are wrong. The dealer will also charge this sneaky fee on a lease (which, here in Florida, goes by at least 22 names according to a state Senate investigative report).

Furthermore, the banks and leasing companies all charge their version of the dealer fee, commonly referred to as the "lease acquisition fee" or "bank fee." It's fairly common for the leasing institutions or companies to kick back half of this to the dealer. This charge averages about $800 or $900.

5. There's a "lease-disposal" fee.

It would almost be funny if it weren't so deceptive.

The bank is charging you an extra fee for leasing you the car and then hitting you again for taking the car back. It certainly incurs a cost for arranging the lease and for taking the lease back, but this is just business overhead and should be included in its price, which is your lease payment.

The motive behind all of this, of course, is the same motive behind the dealer fee. It allows the illusion of a lower price than you are actually paying.

6. **You face higher insurance costs.**

Typically, a bank requires you to carry more insurance on a leased car than you might ordinarily buy if you purchased your car.

Furthermore, the cost of insurance is simply higher on leased cars. That may be because insurance companies know that people are not as careful driving a leased car (belonging to the bank) as they are their own car.

7. **There are higher credit requirements.**

Another reason dealers advertise lease payments is that many people who respond to the ad cannot qualify to lease a car and the dealer then tries to sell them the same car.

Of course the payments are much higher, but the dealer accomplish ed his purpose: He got you in the door.

If you have a credit score below 720 from one or more of the three major credit-reporting agencies in the USA (Equifax, TransUnion and Experian), which many people have, you can probably forget about leasing that car for the "advertised" payment.

You may be able to lease it at a higher payment if you have a 680-plus score, but many people don't and so cannot lease a car at all.

8. **There is no tax advantage to leasing.**

This is not really a booby trap, but a lot of people lease cars thinking they can write off the lease payment faster than they can depreciate a car if they buy it. This is not so. Check with your accountant.

One real advantage I do see to leasing over buying is that you are protected against unexpected depreciation of the vehicle and collision damage.

When a bank or leasing company establishes a lease payment for a particular model car, the single biggest variable is what that car is going to be worth at the end of the lease.

They can't know and they have to guess. If they guess high and the car is worth a lot less at the end of the lease, you have no obligation and the bank can suffer a big loss when they sell it at auction.

This happens more often than you might think. If you had bought the car, you would be the one to worry about the unexpected low trade-in value when you bought your next car.

On the other hand, if the bank guesses that the value of your lease car is lower than what the market value really is, you have an option to purchase that car at this low price. Even if you don't want to keep the car, you could buy the car at this below-market option price, sell it to a dealer for the true higher value and pocket the difference.

On the same subject of "unexpected depreciation," this also occurs if your leased car has collision damage. Any car that has had collision damage depreciates more than one that hasn't. Even if the car is completely repaired and paid by insurance, a car that has been in a major collision will be worth several thousands dollars less. This cost is borne by the leasing company, not by you.

Chapter 32

Don't Be Flipped to a Lease

One of the most popular weapons in car dealers' arsenals is the infamous "lease flip." This is car-dealer jargon for switching a customer who originally intended to buy a car to leasing the car.

Of course, the motivation to do this is more profit for the dealer and a bigger commission to the salesman. That's not to say that leasing a car is always more costly than buying one, but it can be if you're not careful. And not being careful is exactly what happens when a purchase intender becomes a lessee.

Here's how it happens:

You come into the dealership to buy a car. You may have seen the dealer's advertisement in the newspaper or on TV for a particular model.

More than likely, you are prepared to make a down payment and/or trade in your old vehicle. You have a monthly payment in mind because almost everybody has a budget and we usually translate most purchases into whether or not we can fit them into our monthly budgets. You negotiate the best price you can to buy the car or maybe the sale price is good enough.

Now the salesman, or more often, the finance and insurance (F&I) manager or business manager, tells you what your monthly payment will be.

Let's say that you have a trade-in worth $15,000 and aren't going to put any cash down. The F&I manager tells you your monthly payment will be $427 per month.

But that's way more than you can afford and you tell him you can't buy the car because you can't afford a payment that high. He asks you how much you can afford and you tell him it must be under $350 per month. Now he has you set up perfectly for the lease flip.

"Mr. Smith, I think I have just the right thing for you. What would you say if I told you that you can drive that new car home today for just $349 per month?"

You say, with glee, "We have a deal!"

Guess what? You've just been flipped. If you had bought the car at the advertised price or negotiated a very good price, the dealer probably would have made about $1,000 profit and the salesman would have made about a $200 commission. Now that you've let yourself be flipped to a lease, the dealer could be making $15,000 and the salesman could be making a $3,000 commission.

I'm not exaggerating. I get calls weekly from victims of lease flips. Many of the callers are elderly and some of them are widows who'd never bought a car before on their own, but had relied on their husbands.

There's no law that limits the profit that dealers can make when they sell or lease a car. Ten thousand dollars, $15,000 and even $20,000 profits are made—and usually on leases. The dealers can do this by using the trade-in as a "capitalized cost reduction" on the lease but allowing less for the trade than it is actually worth.

In the example above, your trade-in may be worth $15,000, but you were allowed only $5,000 to reduce the capitalized costs of the lease. Also, the dealer could have raised the price of the car you negotiated or the sale price to the manufacturer's suggested retail price (MSRP) or even 110 percent of MSRP, which is allowed by the leasing companies.

By manipulating the number of months of the lease and the down payment (the capitalized cost reduction), a dealer can give you as low a payment as you ask for and still make an exorbitant profit.

Most lessees are so focused on monthly payments that they don't carefully analyze what they are agreeing to and signing. The shorter the number of months of a lease, the greater the impact the down payment has on the monthly payment.

A $5,000 down payment reduces the monthly payment on a 36-month lease by $139 per month, $208 on a 24-month lease and $417 on a 12-month lease.

Incredibly, many victims of the lease flip never thought about the fact that after the 12-, 24- or 36-month term of the lease, they own nothing.

On the other hand, after 36 months, a car with a good resale value should be worth about half of what you paid for it.

Many people who have never leased before mistakenly think they can bring their leased car back early if they want. Leasing is not renting and you can bring your car back early only if you make all of the remaining lease payments.

If you had bought the car for $30,000 and financed it for 36 months, you would have about $15,000 in equity at the end of 36 months and no monthly payments. You were building equity with every monthly payment of the purchase but you were building zero equity with your 36 lease payments.

As I said before, don't let this frighten you from ever leasing a car. Leasing can be a good choice and is sometimes the best choice.

Chapter 33

Should I Buy or Lease?

Unfortunately, as with most things, there is no simple answer to the question of whether you should lease or buy your next car. However, it is important that you evaluate both options, because one or the other usually will have a significant cost advantage.

The most important factor in deciding between a lease and a purchase is the vehicle you choose.

If you are buying a used vehicle, you can pretty much rule out a lease as a viable alternative. Banks and other leasing companies do not offer favorable money factors or residuals on used cars. This would translate into you paying a lot more for a lease.

Ironically, residuals should be relatively higher for used cars. The residual is the percentage of the depreciated value of the car remaining at the end of the lease. A used car experiences the largest portion of its depreciation when it is driven off the showroom floor.

But banks and leasing companies are leery of used cars because they have to rely too heavily on the dealer for the vehicle's true condition and most used cars have no new-car warranty remaining.

If you are getting a new car, the most attractive leases will usually be with makes and models having the highest resale values.

You can check this by comparing the cost of the new car with the wholesale value of a 2-, 3- or 4-year-old model. A good website for this is www.kbb.com, the website for *Kelley Blue Book*. This is how banks and other car-leasing entities calculate their residuals.

The makes with the higher residuals and resale values are the more popular brands, those that don't employ excessive rebates and incentives, and those that don't sell large numbers of cars to rental and leasing companies.

Generally speaking, these are mostly Japanese makes, some European and even some domestic cars that are in high demand and low supply, such as the Chevrolet Corvette.

If you decide to get a new car that has a high resale value, which makes it a good candidate for leasing, be sure that you get lease quotes from several banks, credit unions, leasing companies, etc. The money factor (equivalent to the interest rate in a purchase) and residuals will vary.

You should shop your financing if you are buying and shop your lease rates/residuals if you are leasing.

Many people think there is a tax advantage to leasing. This is not true. You can deduct only that portion of the usage of a car that is for business whether you lease or buy. For a lease, that represents part of the lease payment and for a purchase that represents part of the depreciation.

Here are some things to be careful of if you lease:

1. Your insurance cost will be considerably higher.

2. Do not opt for a lease term beyond the time you want to drive the car. You may be tempted by lower payments on lease terms from 60 to 72 months, but don't do this! You are obligated to pay the leasing company for many more months than you want to keep the car and you would have to pay a very large sum of money to get out of the lease early.

3. Never allow a dealer to switch you from a purchase to a lease at the last minute simply because he offers you a lower payment, a common tactic to raise the profit on the transaction. Remember, at the end of the lease you own nothing, but after the last payment of a purchase, you own the car; so naturally, your lease payment will be lower than a purchase payment.

4. Be sure you understand how many miles per year you will be allowed in your lease before you would begin to accumulate a per-mile charge. Most leases are for 12,000 miles per year. If you drive more miles than this per year, you could be confronted with a very large surprise charge at your lease termination.

5. When you sign your lease, there will be a fee commonly labeled as a "lease acquisition fee." Part of this fee goes to the leasing company but part may go to the dealer and is therefore negotiable. Ask him to waive his portion of the lease acquisition fee because it is part of his profit on the lease.

The cost of a car is the total cost of the car during the time you drove it. If you lease it, that is the sum of the payments. If you buy it, it is the total cost of the depreciation plus interest.

Of course, you will have extraneous costs, such as maintenance, insurance, repairs and fuel, but except for insurance — these are the same for either a lease or a purchase.

Too many people look only at the purchase price of the car. A higher-priced leased car with a higher resale or residual value can actually cost you less than a lower-priced car.

Section Six

SERVICE

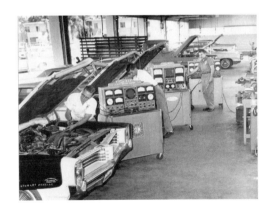

Chapter 34

Eight Rules for Servicing Your Car

You buy a car only once every four or five years, but you should service your car at least two or three times a year.

Car dealers make more money from servicing and repairing cars than selling them. The person who takes your order when you drive into a service lane is paid on commission, just like the salesperson who sold you your car.

His title may be service adviser, service writer or assistant service manager, but he's really a salesman. The more service or repairs he sells you, the more money he earns.

Adhere to these eight easy-to-follow rules and you will not get taken to the cleaners and still get the service necessary to keep your car running well.

1. **Always ask for a written estimate.** A number of states have laws that give you the right to receive a written estimate for your service and repairs. If the estimate exceeds the actual amount by greater than a certain percentage (10 percent in Florida), you don't have to pay that overage.

Be sure that you get a written, not verbal, estimate. If you're contacted later and told there is additional work that should be done, ask that it be put in writing, too. If you're not in the dealership, ask someone to text, email or fax this before you approve it.

2. **Insist the technician or service adviser test-drive your car with you.** If you have a drivability problem—meaning squeaks, rattles, pulling, vibration, inadequate braking, etc.—always insist that you accompany the tech (preferably) or service adviser on a test drive so that he or she can be an eyewitness to your complaint.

Repeat this test drive after the work has been completed. Descriptions of drivability problems are often miscommunicated verbally and in writing. The service adviser and technicians will usually not offer the test drive because it's time-consuming and they're paid on commission. It's up to you to insist.

3. **Request the best technician to work on your car.** Most service departments have several techs who can work on your car. Some are better than others, just like doctors, lawyers and hair stylists.

Why should your car be repaired or serviced by the guy that just happens to be waiting for the next job? There's an old joke that can be applied to this: "What do you call a doctor who graduated last in his medical school class?

Answer: A doctor!"

The first time you visit a service department, ask who the top tech is. He or she usually has been working there longer, attended more schools and holds more ASE (National Institute for Automotive Service Excellence certification) ratings.

The service advisers and service manager know exactly who these are and usually will be glad to tell you, especially if it determines whether or not they will keep you as a service customer.

4. **Request the best service adviser.** You choose your service adviser pretty much the same way you choose your technician: experience, training, certifications, etc. There's an additional measurement that's very important with a service adviser, the customer satisfaction score.

All manufacturers that I know of grade service advisers on how well they individually treat their customers. The sum of these scores is the dealer's scorecard to the factory and very important to him. You have to ask for this score; it's not usually made public.

Once you've picked your technician and service adviser, you're going to have to make an appointment to be sure they are both available on the day and time you bring your car in.

Having both of them handle your service will require some flexibility on your part and may require longer for the work to be completed. But this is a small price to pay for the work to be done right the first time and for the work to be something that was truly necessary.

5. __Get competitive estimates on repair work.__ Repair work is work that you don't regularly require—for example, if your air conditioner, radio or transmission is broken—that is what you have to be careful about. Dealers typically price oil changes, tire rotations and balance and front-end alignments competitively.

Repair work, because you're not familiar with the price, is where you have to watch out. When you get your first estimate on an expensive repair, get at least two more from two other service departments.

Often the mere act of "shopping" the original price will cause the first estimator to lower his. In fact, if you feel comfortable with the service department that gave you the first estimate because you like the tech and the service adviser, offer to let them repair your car if they will meet the lower price.

6. __Know which maintenance is recommended by your car's manufacturer.__ If you don't read anything else in your car's owner's manual, read what the manufacturer recommends for maintenance. Service departments typically recommend far more maintenance than the manufacturer does. Usually they don't tell you this unless you ask, hoping that you will assume that their recommended maintenance is the same.

Manufacturers will usually say that for extreme or unusual operating conditions (stop-and-go driving, very high or low temperatures, etc.), additional maintenance may be required. You must be the judge of this, but for a rule of thumb, you can't go too far wrong following the manufacturer's recommendations.

7. __Have your car's vehicle identification number (VIN) checked occasionally for manufacturer's bulletins.__ All dealers should run your VIN through their computer at least once a year to be sure there are no outstanding recall campaigns or technical advisory bulletins. In fact, if you require a repair, you should always ask them to check to see if the factory may cover it when it would otherwise be out of warranty.

Be aware that sometimes dealers are prohibited by the manufacturer from telling their customers about a bulletin unless the customer asks. There are so many bulletins that come out all the time that many dealers are overwhelmed.

If you are having your car fixed at an independent shop, you should be very careful about this because independent shops would be unlikely to have any knowledge of these. Your best bet is to check on the Internet for bulletins on your particular car, model, and year.

8. Don't take no for an answer when your car is out of warranty. If your car is just one day or one mile out of warranty, it will usually be covered anyway. This principle applies to a few hundred miles and a few months, too. But you have to ask and often insist. Performing free work out of warranty is referred to as "goodwill." Some dealers have the ability to do this and all manufacturers do. If the dealer tells you no, ask him to contact the factory service representative.

For more specific details, see the chapter What Can You Do When Your Car Is Out of Warranty?

Chapter 35

Who is Best to Service Your Car, Your Dealer or an Independent Shop?

Should you, or must you, take your car back to a dealer for service?

I can answer the second half of that question easily. No, you do not have to take your car to a dealership's service department for maintenance or repairs, unless the repairs are among those covered under your car's warranty.

Be advised, however, that the manufacturer has the right to take into consideration how well you maintained your car in accordance with the recommendations spelled out in your owner's manual when approving warranty repairs. If you do choose an independent service facility, be sure it performs the maintenance as recommended in your owner's manual. Also, be sure that you keep a record of that maintenance.

Whether or not you should choose an independent facility is more complicated. The fact that about 75 percent of most new-car buyers don't bring their cars back to their dealer for service is a huge problem for all manufacturers and car dealers.

It's a problem for manufacturers because they can lose the parts sales, which include oil filters and oil. The profit margin on auto parts is much higher than on the car itself. If you added up the price of all the parts in your car ($20,000 to $30,000), the total would be many times the price you paid for it.

It's also a problem for dealers. The retail markup on an auto part is at least 40 percent and your car's markup is less than half of that. The average dealer makes more money selling parts than he does cars, and also makes more money selling the labor to service and repair cars than in selling cars.

In most dealerships, the new-car department loses money or makes relatively little. The parts and service departments are the real moneymakers.

Finally, a customer who does bring his vehicle back to the dealer for service is twice as likely to buy his next car from that dealer.

The reasons car buyers don't usually bring their cars back to the dealer for service are, very simply, price and convenience.

Independent service facilities and fast-lube shops are more plentiful than dealers and there's usually one closer than a dealership. Why drive 20 miles to your dealer for an oil change when there's a quick-lube shop around the corner?

Prices are usually less at independent service facilities. Independents have lower overheads and generally don't use original factory parts. Non-factory parts, often manufactured overseas, are usually less expensive than original factory parts. Independents frequently don't have to pay their technicians as much as dealers do.

To combat this problem, many manufacturers are offering free maintenance on new cars for two years and even longer. The idea is to get the new-car buyer into the habit of coming back to the dealer.

The dealer also has the opportunity to sell the customer some services that aren't included in the free maintenance package. Dealers are also offering such amenities as free oil changes, and a very few even offer free tires and batteries as long as customers have all factory-recommended services done by them.

I know I still haven't answered the question of whether you should bring your car back to the dealer. I would recommend that you do but the answer can depend on how good the dealer's service department is.

However, most car dealers have better-trained technicians and more and better diagnostic equipment than the average independent.

Furthermore, the dealer's technicians are specialists in the brand of car or cars sold there. A Ford dealer's technicians, for example, know more about Fords than a Chevrolet dealer's technicians and more than the average independent technician. For this reason, I usually recommend that you bring your car to a dealer of that brand for the more expensive, difficult repairs.

Good, independent technicians can change the oil and rotate and balance the tires on any car. But they can't always diagnose a transmission problem and, if they could, may not have the specialized tools needed to fix it.

If the dealer of your brand is not price competitive, by all means, check out independent service companies. But be sure the technician—sometimes the owner is the technician—has the proper training.

He or she should have certifications from the National Institute for Automotive Service Excellence, ASE. There are ASE certifications for all components of the car, including air-conditioning, engine and transmission. Ask to see his or her certification and be sure that it's up to date.

Check the company out with the Better Business Bureau, the county office of consumer affairs and the attorney general's office. Ask for the names of references from existing customers. Be sure the technician is bonded so that, in the event you have a claim, you will be paid. Find out how long the company has been in business.

Two things to be on guard against, with both dealers and independents, are the "up-sell" and hidden charges. When you see an ad for a $16.95 oil change, you can be assured that you won't leave that service department paying only $16.95.

The oil change includes a "free inspection," which means the commissioned technician and service adviser will look for anything else that may need maintenance or fixing on your car.

Just be sure what they recommend is really needed; the safest way is to take it somewhere else for a second opinion.

Also, watch out for that hidden, extra charge at the bottom of your service invoice. It goes by many different names. Some of the most common are sundry supplies, environmental impact fee, hazardous waste disposal fee, supplies and small tools. This is nothing more than profit to the dealer and is calculated by adding a percentage of the total invoice, usually 5 or 10 percent.

Almost all dealers and independents add this charge or charges, which should be made illegal. My advice is to refuse to pay it and, in most cases, they will agree to remove it from your bill.

Chapter 36

Misaligned Wheels are Silent Tire Killers

Estimates on the number of cars on the road right now that need an alignment range from as low as 25 percent to as high as 75 percent!

Even if you have the best tires and vehicle that money can buy, all it takes is a little pothole or curb to cost you a new set of tires.

If you live, or do a lot of driving, in an area with unpaved roads or lots of roads in need of repair and/or being repaired, you're especially vulnerable to potholes and other road obstacles that can knock your front and rear wheels out of alignment.

One of my favorite ways to misalign my wheels has to do with curbs. I can't seem to avoid them when I'm parking, especially when backing into a parallel parking place.

Most people know that if their car is pulling to the left or right, they need an alignment. Most also know that if they see wear on the edges of their tires, they may have an alignment problem (it could also be under-inflated tires).

But what most people don't know is that your wheels can be badly out of alignment with no symptoms whatsoever.

It's like high blood pressure in that respect and that's why I used the phrase "silent tire killer." Some people can tell their blood pressure is high from headaches or dizziness but the majority feel no symptoms.

Most people learn they have hypertension only when their doctor measures their blood pressure. Unfortunately, some never find out until it's too late.

At one point, I had to replace a set of tires that had only about 5,000 miles on them because all four of my wheels were out of alignment.

There were no symptoms whatsoever. My car didn't pull, my steering wheel was perfectly straight and I saw no abnormal tire wear.

I had brought my car in for its routine 5,000-mile service and when my technician put it up on the lift to rotate and balance my wheels and tires, he found that the inside was severely worn on all four tires.

When you have offsetting misalignment on opposing wheels, there is no pull and when the wear is only on the inside of the tire, it's invisible until the car is up on a lift.

I'd had my car aligned only a few months earlier, but I had knocked it out of alignment again without even realizing it. When you buy a new or used car, you should always insist that the dealer check the alignment. A new car can be knocked out of alignment in many ways. Transporting the car to the dealer from the manufacturer and driving it on or off a ship, truck or train can do it. A technician can do it during a pre-delivery road test or a car salesman or prospective customer might during a test drive.

Cars may have their wheels knocked out of alignment as well when being traded back and forth between dealers. In fact, the tires on your new car could actually be misaligned even before it leaves the manufacturer's plant! It's not something most people would even consider.

As you can see, there are lots of reasons a new car could need a wheel alignment. Because it has so few miles on it, though, it's almost impossible for you to notice the misalignment from uneven tire wear.

And remember that a demonstration drive in a new or used car won't necessarily reveal any symptoms such as pull or abnormal tire wear.

Because of this possibility, it's a good idea to insist on an alignment check—and at no charge—before you even drive your new car off the lot. If the wheels are not aligned property, realignment should be covered under your warranty.

You should ask for a copy of the computer printout showing the specific measurements before and after your alignment.

You should have your alignment checked every time you bring your car in for service, approximately every six months or 5,000 miles. If you hit a curb, pothole or other obstacle in the road or notice abnormal wear on the edge of your tires, bring it in for an alignment check immediately.

Selling a customer a new car with wheels that are misaligned and not allowing that car to be aligned under warranty is simply not right. The consequences of this can be not only very expensive for the customer but a potential safety issue as well.

Thus, you should insist that the dealer and manufacturer who sold you your car prove to you that your wheels are aligned properly. Make this a written condition of the purchase.

Ideally, all new cars should have their alignments checked just before they are delivered to the customer. Many dealers might encounter a problem with reimbursement by the manufacturer for doing this and that's why it's not already being done.

Chapter 37

Modern Wheel Alignment Requires Modern Technology

Manufacturers consider alignment a maintenance item that is your responsibility. This is why it's important to be sure your new car is aligned when your car is still within the alignment warranty time and mileage.

There are manufacturers that allow one alignment under warranty for a short time and mileage period—one year or 20,000 miles—but some will only permit the dealer to check your alignment if you complain about pull or abnormal tire wear.

When the service department measures your alignment, be sure it uses the latest equipment. A modern alignment machine is computerized, measures all four wheels, and requires that your car be elevated on the lift and that the technician be fully trained.

Aligning the four wheels of your car, like everything else, is a lot more complicated than it used to be. Cars' shocks and suspensions are more complex today. When most cars had rear-wheel drive, aligning was simple.

Now we have mostly front-wheel drive and even some all-wheel drive cars on the road. We no longer do just front-end alignments; we have to align all four wheels.

In the old days, service departments routinely checked the alignment for all cars that drove in. There was a simple machine built into the service drive that registered the measurements when you drove over the track. Some service departments still use these dinosaurs, but they are not accurate on today's cars.

There are three basic measurements that must be exactly right for your tires to be in alignment: castor, camber and toe-in. The website www.tirekiller.com links to a video that gives a very clear, easy-to-understand explanation of these measurements. The video was produced by Hunter, which is the largest and best manufacturer of alignment machines in the world.

Nowadays, many alignment machines are so complex that it takes almost as long to measure your alignment as to adjust it. For this reason, many service departments will charge you the same to measure your alignment as they do to actually align it, even if the measurements indicate it is perfectly in adjustment.

There are newer, very expensive machines that will quickly measure alignments but most service departments don't have these. Because this state-of-the-art equipment runs about $60,000, many independent service departments and even some dealers can't afford it.

If your dealer doesn't have a computerized, up-to-date alignment system, consider going somewhere that does.

Fortunately, this is the kind of machine we now use at our dealership. Because it is so efficient, and because alignments checks can now be done so quickly, we don't charge our customers for alignments checks anymore.

I invested in my new Hunter alignment machine because it allows me to check an alignment in less than 10 minutes. This permits me to check a customer's alignment at no charge, but has another bonus.

It also makes it fast and easy now to check the wheel alignments of every car that comes through my service drive (about 100 each day), including all my company cars, my parts delivery trucks, my service courtesy vans, my new car demonstrators and my used cars.

Consequently, I've collected some astounding data since I began checking every car for alignment.

About one car out of every four I checked was out of alignment, which didn't surprise me that much; industry data support this. But what did surprise me is the fact that about one out of four new cars is also out of alignment! I'm defining a new car as one under a year old or 20,000 miles.

As I wrote in the last chapter, one of the tangible symptoms for misalignment is pulling to the left or right. But all it takes is two adjustments on two different wheels to be out in opposite directions to cancel each other out—in which case there are no revealing pulls.

Now here are the shocking facts I recognized when I began checking the wheel alignment on all new cars that come through my service drive.

Before I purchased the Hunter alignment machine, I checked and aligned a new car only when the customer complained of a pull or uneven tire wear. The average number of alignments I checked and fixed each month was only seven.

Now that I'm checking the measurements on all new cars, I'm aligning an average of 46 monthly, an increase of 650 percent! This means that for every wheel alignment I corrected previously, there were six more that were not detected and fixed.

Many of my previous customers ended up paying for an alignment that should have been covered by the warranty and many may have had to replace tires sooner than they should have.

It pains me to admit that I hadn't been checking my customers' new cars for alignments before. In spite of my years in the car business, I really had no idea of the extent of new cars sold that were out of alignment.

Also, I really didn't have a choice, for two reasons. It was hugely expensive to pay a technician the lengthy labor time required with my old alignment equipment, and the manufacturer would not pay for an alignment check or alignment on a new car unless the customer complained of a pull or uneven tire wear.

This is common practice with most, if not all, manufacturers, and I believe it's a huge mistake.

Chapter 38

What Can You Do if Your Warranty Has Run Out?

Most everyone has heard these words: "I'm sorry but you'll have to pay for this repair because your car is out of the manufacturer's warranty."

What should you say or do? Obviously, we're not talking about cars that are way out of warranty. A 10-year-old vehicle with 200,000 miles on it and a three-year or 36,000-mile warranty will not be repaired without charge by your dealer or manufacturer.

However, for those cars that are close to being within the warranty time and mileage there is a good chance that you can persuade the dealer/manufacturer to pay at least a portion of the cost of repair. This chapter is designed to tell you how to accomplish this.

The easiest way to have your car repaired at no cost is if you initially brought the vehicle in for a problem while it was still under warranty and the dealer "attempted" to fix it, but did not. When the problem resurfaces, as long as you have in writing and on the record that the attempt was made, you should have no problem getting your car repaired at no charge.

To the lesser degree that your car is out of warranty, the greater your chance is of having the factory authorize a "goodwill" repair. Goodwill is what they call all repairs made at no charge when the car is out of warranty. If your car is only five miles out of warranty, this should be very easy to have approved. The further out of warranty it is, however, the more difficult this becomes and the less likely that you will have 100 percent of the cost paid by the manufacturer.

For example, a car that's 3,000 miles out of a 36,000-mile warranty may be granted just 50 percent of the cost of the repair under goodwill.

It's important to understand that the dealer often has no say in whether an out-of-warranty car can be repaired under goodwill. A good dealer should support your request for it, however, because the manufacturer would pay him for doing the repair and this would also make his customer happy.

On the other hand, a bad dealer may not support your request because he can charge you more than what the factory would reimburse him. Dealers are reimbursed by manufacturers at a capped rate for labor and parts for warranty and goodwill repairs. But they can charge any amount they can get you to agree to pay for all other repairs.

If a dealer is reluctant to support your request for goodwill, be sure to take your request all the way to top. Take it to the service manager, then to the general manager and then to the owner.

If the dealer won't support you, try taking it to another dealer who will. It's very important that you have the support of the dealer when you take your request to the manufacturer. Without it, it's highly unlikely you will get help.

Some dealers are granted the authority to make goodwill adjustments directly, as well as to make decisions as to whether a repair should be covered under warranty. This can be both good and bad.

As I said earlier, a dealer can have an ulterior motive for not wanting to repair your car under warranty. He can make more money if he makes you pay. A dealer who is authorized to make warranty/goodwill decisions is so authorized because he has kept his warranty and goodwill costs low. This is bad for the customer if the way he has kept them low is by denying legitimate claims to make himself look good in the eyes of the factory.

To some service managers, it's more important to be popular with the factory than with the dealer he works for. You want a service manager who works for a good dealer and whose loyalty is with that dealer and to his customers.

Manufacturers and dealers will favor customers who have bought cars from them and had their cars serviced with them. The dealer/manufacturer has your entire sales and service history on record. If you have bought two or more cars of this make and had them serviced regularly by dealers of that make, it is more likely that they will stretch on the warranty coverage and goodwill.

When asking for repairs for your car when it is out of warranty, be courteous, factual and as brief as possible. Never threaten to take your business away, sue or call the media. Never raise your voice or curse. Dealership and factory employees are just like you. They tend to respond more positively to someone who is courteous and rational.

You should put your request in writing, email or regular mail. If things are moving too slowly, it's a good idea to call the factory's toll-free customer assistance number. Your request will be referred back to the dealer, but it's good to be on record with the factory.

When encountering difficulties, go online and research your repair problem. Google and other online resources will direct you to blogs and other sources of information about people who have the same problem. You will be amazed at the number of people who do and who may be able to offer potential solutions.

Sometimes even your dealer may not be aware that this repair is common among owners of the same year, make and model. Knowing this gives you a strong psychological advantage.

When you research your repair problem, you might find out that the manufacturer has issued a notice to its dealers about it. This kind of notice is referred to as a TSB or technical service bulletin. Sometimes a TSB will authorize the dealer to repair the car under warranty but only if the customer asks. You may even learn this repair is covered under a recall campaign, although the dealer should have known that when he checked your VIN in his computer.

The bottom line is: Don't just take no for an answer. Go through the steps that I've covered above and you should have a pretty good chance of getting at least some of your repair paid for by the manufacturer.

Chapter 39

Why New Car Tires Wear Out So Fast

The tires that came with your last new car were not designed by Michelin, Goodyear, Bridgestone or any other tire manufacturer. They were designed by the manufacturer of your car. If your new car came with a set of Michelins, Michelin made the tire, but they made it to the specifications set by your car manufacturer. Furthermore, your auto manufacturer does not warranty the tires on your new car even though he tells you that you have a "bumper to bumper" warranty.

The last time I checked, my tires were between my front and rear bumpers. Even though GM, for example, designed the tires on your Chevrolet, it has no responsibility if they are defective. The tire manufacturer bears that responsibility.

The OEM (original equipment manufacturer) tires that came with your car can't be replaced after they've worn out — which is a good thing.

And they will wear out much sooner than they should. This is because virtually all auto manufacturers specify very soft rubber, which means they wear out too fast.

Why would the manufacturers do that? They want that new car to have the smoothest ride possible, even at the expense of your having to buy a new set of tires at half the mileage you would expect.

When you test-drive that brand-new car and it rides very, very smoothly, you're more likely to buy it. You'll find out how fast the tires wear out much later, and when you do, you'll blame it on the tire maker.

By the way, another way carmakers delude you into thinking your ride is very smooth is by recommending low tire inflation. The number you see on your doorjamb or in your car's owners manual is the car manufacturer's recommended air pressure. The number on your tire is the tire maker's recommendation.

The number on the doorjamb is the minimum and the number on the tire is the maximum. There's typically a 10-pound difference. I recommend you try the maximum and, if the ride's too rough, split the difference. You'll not only get longer tire wear but better gas mileage.

I can't prove it, but I suspect another reason auto manufacturers design their own tires is to cut costs. By cutting a few corners in the design and specifications, they can increase their profits and cut the overall car price.

Think about it. GM sells roughly 9 million cars each year. If the company can design a tire that costs $5 less to manufacture, that's $20 per car (not counting the spare) or $180 million going right to the bottom line!

If the purpose was to design a better tire, why not make these OEM tires available for the car owner to buy after the first set wears out?

Many car owners think they're replacing the Firestones or Michelins that were on their new car with the same version of the tire, but they're not. The tire might be the same size and look the same, but it's a different model number.

One thing you should look for on your first set of replacement tires is the "tread-wear index," which is molded into the side of your tires. This number will be 200 to 800.

Your OEM tires will have a lower number because they're made of softer rubber. If the tires that came on your car had a 200-tread wear index and you replaced them with 400, you should get twice the mileage on your second set of tires.

The car might not ride as smoothly, but most people don't notice the difference. And to my way of thinking, cutting your tires' cost in half by having them last twice as long is pretty good compensation for a slightly rougher ride.

When replacing your tires, don't get enamored by a sexy brand name. Brands aren't always built on quality but also on advertising.

Also, a famous-brand tire makes all different kinds of tires with many different designs and specifications. Just because it's "a Michelin" doesn't necessarily mean it's a good tire. If Michelin made that tire for an auto manufacturer who designed the tire with only two things in mind, low cost and soft ride, you didn't get a very good tire.

My recommendation is to check *Consumer Reports* for the best tire replacements. You'll find tire brands recommended that you've probably never heard about. The Japanese and Chinese make some very good tires, but they have different-sounding names and chances are you won't see them advertised heavily on TV.

Chapter 40

Coping with the Body Shop and Insurance Companies

I guess one of the worst things that can happen to us in our driving experience is to be involved in an accident. Even when there are no injuries, we still have to cope with our auto insurance company and maybe the other party's auto insurance company.

We also have to select a body shop or accept the one recommended by our insurance company. After you notify your insurance company of your accident, this is your first big decision. Choosing the right body shop is every bit as important as selecting the right doctor or dentist, except that it's your car that's being worked on, not your body or teeth.

Most of the time, your insurance company will recommend a body shop. Consider its recommendation but also do your own due diligence—because if you choose your own body shop, then that body shop is working for you and is your advocate, not your insurance company's advocate.

Remember that your insurance company is the one paying for your repairs and one of its most important considerations is the cost of repairing your car.

The insurance company, of course, should also be interested in a quality repair, but cost is at least an equal consideration.

Your No. 1 concern should be quality, not cost. Your insurance company may tell you it's OK to have your car repaired at the body shop of your choice, but it won't guarantee the quality of the repairs if you take it someplace other than where they recommend.

While a reputable body shop should guarantee its own repairs, what this means is that you could be on your own if, for example, newly applied paint started to peel and the work had not been done by the insurance-recommended shop.

I strongly recommend that you give first consideration to a body shop owned by a franchised dealer of the make of your car. This body shop will have the advantage of faster availability of factory parts, more experience repairing your make and model, and its technicians will usually be better trained in repairing your make of car.

Obviously, a car that has been damaged and repaired is worth less than one that has not. Even with a quality repair, a late-model car with substantial repairs could be worth thousands of dollars less when you trade it in. This sad fact is a very good reason you should be sure that your car is ruled a "total" by your insurance company if it meets the criteria.

A car that will cost 70 percent of its current market value to repair is usually considered a total, and your insurance company should replace your car, not repair it.

If it's a close call, resulting in a decision to repair the vehicle, you should get a second opinion. This is the time when it's good to have a body shop that you chose that is beholden to you and not to your insurance company.

Your insurance policy will dictate the parts the insurance company may use in repairing your car. It is highly desirable to use OEM parts (parts manufactured by or for the company that built your car) as opposed to "after-market" parts, often manufactured in Taiwan or another foreign country.

These parts are copies of OEM parts and much cheaper than the genuine parts. They may not fit as well or have the correct tolerances. You should find out before you purchase your policy if it will provide for OEM parts.

If the company you already have car insurance with won't authorize OEM parts, however, ask if you can pay the difference. It is worth the investment.

It is very difficult to forecast accurately the time it will take to complete a major repair. This is because there is usually hidden damage that is impossible to detect until the car has been disassembled.

When hidden damage is detected, the body shop must call your insurance company's adjustor to authorize supplemental work. This work may require parts that were not anticipated in the initial repair that have to be ordered. There is no one to blame for this; it's just a fact of collision repair.

The bottom line: Expect delays when your car is having a major repair. A quality body shop will "under-promise and over-deliver" by building in some extra time to allow for the inevitable supplemental repairs.

Be sure you understand what degree of rental-reimbursement coverage is included in your insurance policy. It varies from policy to policy. Some have no rental car reimbursement whatsoever, some have partial and some have complete coverage. During a major repair, you could be without your car for more than a month.

In summary, choose your insurance company carefully and read your policy closely before you commit to purchasing auto insurance.

Choose your body shop just as carefully. You need a quality body shop owned by the franchised dealer for your make of car that will be an advocate for your interests more than for your insurance company.

Chapter 41

Cheap Oil Changes Can Cost You in the Long Run

The container that holds your engine oil underneath your car is made of very thin sheet metal, often aluminum. Because the bottom of the oil pan is so thin, the opening that technicians use to drain your oil cannot hold very many threads.

The oil plug, which is removed and replaced every time your oil is changed, clings to those few threads.

Manufacturers do this mainly because they're trying to make your car as light as possible in order to meet fuel economy requirements. Then too, the less metal there is in a part, the cheaper it is.

It might sound unreasonable when you think about how little it would cost to have an oil pan that was just one quarter-inch thicker, but multiply this by tens of thousands of parts on a car and pretty soon you're talking lots of weight and lots of money.

Depending on the make and model of your car, you can expect the threads to wear out on your oil pan as early as 40,000 miles just from normal wear and tear. It can be sooner or later than that depending on how often you change your oil.

Unfortunately, when this happens, there's not a safe resolution to the problem other than replacing your entire oil pan. This can cost anywhere from $150 to $350, depending on the make and model.

There are plenty of less-expensive solutions some people suggest—such as oversized plugs, rubber plugs and re-threading—but they are not 100 percent effective.

If you gamble with one of these less-successful solutions and the rubber plug pops out, you're looking at buying a new engine for thousands of dollars. In modern cars you have only a few seconds to stop an engine that is losing its oil, which is exactly what happens when the plug drops out. As I'm sure you must know, an engine that loses all of its oil—which is its lifeblood—will not run for long.

As if this isn't enough to concern you, the technician who changes your oil can easily strip the threads in the oil pan by over-tightening the oil plug.

If this happens, you probably won't know about it until you change your oil again and maybe not for several more oil changes.

Stripping threads isn't necessarily an all-or-nothing event. Repeatedly over-tightening the drain plug slightly will cause the threads to wear out prematurely.

Each manufacturer has a specification for exactly how tight the oil plug must be in the oil pan. It's measured in foot-pounds of torque and a typical spec would be 18 FP. If the plug isn't tightened enough, it might fall out, which unfortunately sometimes motivates a technician to over-tighten the plug just to be safe.

If the plug is too loose and falls out, it could cost him his job. To be sure that the oil plug is tightened exactly right, the technician must use a torque wrench, which shows the foot-pounds of torque that the plug has been tightened to.

Believe it or not, many technicians still don't use torque wrenches. Without one, they are just guessing how tight your oil plug is. This is a good reason for you to be very careful about who changes your oil. Don't be shy—specifically ask the service department that changes your oil if the technicians use torque wrenches.

It wouldn't be a bad idea either to find out the manufacturer's specification for torquing your oil drain plug. It shouldn't be necessary if you have your oil changed by the dealer, but it might be if you use an independent service company or quick-lube company.

The person who changes your oil is the usually the lowest-paid individual in that service department. He's called a "lube tech," generally a starting position for an auto technician. The turnover in this position is much greater than for regular mechanical technicians.

I'm sure you can understand why this puts you at risk for not having the job done right.

Be very leery of advertising that promotes cheap oil changes. It's fine to save money having your car serviced, but you should be sure that the person working on your car knows what he is doing and uses the proper tools. He must know the manufacturer's specifications for tightening your particular oil plug and he must use a torque wrench.

Ideally, you should find a trustworthy, knowledgeable lube technician and always have him perform all your oil changes. That way, if there's ever a question about who over-torqued or under-torqued your oil plug, there's only one person who can be held to blame.

Chapter 42

Good People Make Good Car Dealerships

It's important that you carefully choose the individual who advises you and sells you service on your car. These individuals are really commissioned salespeople who sell you service, just like car salespeople sell you cars.

Unfortunately, most dealerships call them something else, such as assistant service manager or service adviser.

In my dealership, we used to call them assistant service managers because that's the term that Toyota uses. We now call them service advisers because too many people thought they were dealing with the service manager.

In all candor, I'd feel more comfortable naming them what they are, "service salespeople," and I may make that change.

Whichever car dealership you choose, take the time to pick and choose those individuals you deal with. Car dealerships, just like other organizations, are nothing more than the sum of their parts: their people.

You should get to know the person who sells you service and if you don't like and trust him or her, ask for another person to handle your service requirements. You should also meet and cultivate a relationship with a manager in the service department.

The same holds true for the sales department. When you buy a car, don't settle for the first salesperson that approaches you. For example, if you're a woman you may feel more comfortable dealing with another woman.

Or, if your native language is Spanish or Creole, you may feel more comfortable with someone who can converse with you in your native tongue.

Don't be shy about asking and don't feel bad about hurting the feelings of the first salesperson. An automobile is the second-largest purchase most people make and it's very important that you feel comfortable with the person selling it to you.

Furthermore, if after dealing with your salesperson for a while you think you made a bad choice, ask to speak to the sales manager or general manager. Believe me, car buyers hold all the cards in today's shaky economy and no sane sales manager is going to lose a sale because a prospective customer doesn't like or trust the salesperson she's dealing with. He will handle your sale personally or choose another salesperson you do feel good about.

Car dealerships have other departments, including parts, finance and insurance, and accounting, and some have body shops. My same recommendation applies to all departments.

A word of caution—when you ask to speak to a manager, be sure you're really speaking to one. Car dealerships are notorious for calling rank-and-file employees managers to trick the customer.

I readily admit that there are no perfect companies, especially car dealerships, and that includes mine. I employ 146 individuals and I would be less than candid if I didn't say I have a few rotten apples in my barrel.

Unfortunately, I don't know who they are and finding them is a continuous work in progress. The same thing applies to all companies.

Even in dealerships recommended to you, there are some employees who would take advantage of you—but most would not. In those dealerships that you may be warned to stay away from, there may also be a few honest, courteous employees.

Then there are all the dealerships that fall somewhere in the middle. Your odds of finding the right individual are much better if you patronize a good company or car dealership, but don't totally let your guard down.

In every organization there's a tipping point. A great company reaches a critical mass of good employees and as its reputation grows, more good employees from other companies seek to be employed there. Honest, hardworking, courteous people enjoy working in an environment where others are like them.

The same holds true for unscrupulous dealerships and bad companies. A good person with a conscience has a very difficult time functioning in an environment where, from top management all the way down, the design is to trick and take advantage of customers. These few good people don't last long in unethical dealerships and flee to a place where they can treat their customers in a manner that lets them sleep at night.

Chapter 43

Commonly Asked Service Questions

Every few months at my dealership, we invite everyone who recently purchased used or new vehicles from us to our new-owners event. Our customers enjoy a buffet dinner and meet my service manager, parts manager, top technician, and my wife, Nancy, and me. There are a lot of questions. Here are the six most frequently asked questions, with my answers:

Q. What grade of gasoline should I use?

A. Use the grade of gasoline recommended by your manufacturer. Most cars run just fine on regular, but those with the higher-compression engines, and all V-8s, require high-test. There is absolutely no value to using a higher-test, more expensive gas than your car's manufacturer recommends.

You can experiment with using a lower octane than the manufacturer recommends. If you don't hear an engine knock, go ahead with the lower octane, lower-cost gasoline. Manufacturers sometimes recommend higher octane than is really necessary.

Q. What brand of gasoline should I buy?

A. I recommend that you stick with major national brands and avoid the independents. If you buy from Sunoco, Amoco, Mobil, etc., you are far less likely to get contaminated gasoline. Condensation and debris in your gas can cause some very expensive repairs.

I also recommend that you buy your gas from the same gas station as often as possible. That way, if you do have a problem, you will know exactly where it happened. Gas stations that do a high volume and regularly refill their tanks are less likely to have condensation or debris in their tanks.

Q. If I don't put very many miles on my car, do I still need to bring it in every six months for service?

A.The first recommended service is usually after six months or 5,000 miles. Even if you have driven only 1,000 miles in six months, you should bring it in to have your oil changed, your tires checked and your car inspected.

Time is as big a cause of wear on your car as is mileage, especially in extreme climates or conditions where high humidity, intense heat or cold, turbulent weather, very dry or salty air, and even road construction dust, can all take a toll.

Q. How often should I check my tire pressure?

A. Having the correct tire pressure is one of the most underrated maintenance requirements on a car. Not only will maintaining correct tire pressure maximize the life of your tires but it will also increase your gas mileage and make your car safer to drive by improving the braking and handling. Check your tire pressure at least once every month.

Q. How important is it to have my car serviced by the dealer rather than an independent garage?

A. If you have a trusted mechanic or you are a competent "do-it-your-selfer," there is nothing wrong with having routine maintenance, such as oil changes and tire rotations, done outside of your car dealership. I do recommend that you bring it to your dealer for check-ups periodically and always for any kind of repair. Today's automobile is not "your father's automobile." It is a very sophisticated, highly complex, computerized machine.

Factory-authorized dealers must invest hundreds of thousands of dollars in computerized diagnostic machinery and maintain a staff of highly trained technicians who specialize in that make of car.

Q. Should I use regular or synthetic oil?

A. As long as you change your oil at least every 5,000 miles or six months—whichever comes first—you cannot go wrong with either. Synthetic oils are much more expensive than regular oils and are touted as superior by some. I have heard pundits on both sides of this issue. If you choose to use synthetic oil because you believe it is better, be sure that you still change your oil at least every 5,000 miles or six months.

Chapter 44

Pitfalls to Avoid When Having
Your Car Serviced

Before I get into the pitfalls, it is important for you to understand how essential it is to have your car serviced according to the manufacturer's recommendations. The pitfalls and consequences of not doing so can be equal to or greater than those you might experience at the hands of an incompetent or unethical service department.

I do recommend that you have your car serviced and repaired by a franchised dealer of the make of your vehicle. I know that this statement, coming from a franchised car dealer, may be met with some skepticism.

Listen to my reasons before passing judgment.

Modern vehicles are highly complex, computerized machines requiring very sophisticated diagnostic equipment and highly trained technicians. The evolution of new, expensive diagnostic equipment requires constant updating. The evolution of car technology requires continuing education of dealers' factory-trained technicians, who attend many weeks of school every year.

Forty years ago, it was possible for a really good mechanic to fix anybody's car. Those days are gone and your car needs a highly trained specialist with the very latest diagnostic equipment. It is impossible for an independent service company to be competent in servicing and repairing all makes of automobiles.

Carefully choose the dealership that will service your car. You do not have to take your car to the dealership that sold you the car for warranty repairs, as many people believe. Every dealership of your make car will welcome your warranty and non-warranty work.

Do your homework on which dealer has the best service department. Every dealer is graded in customer satisfaction by the manufacturer. Ask to see a copy of the dealer's customer satisfaction index scores. If the dealer does not let you see them, consider taking your business elsewhere.

Check with the Better Business Bureau and the county office of consumer affairs.

When you take your car in for maintenance or repairs, always ask for a written estimate. Most state laws limit the amount a service department can exceed written estimates by a certain percentage — for example, here in Florida it's 10 percent.

When paying your bill, scrutinize the detail to be sure that you know exactly what each charge means. Most service departments add a fee on top of everything else with various labels like "miscellaneous supplies," "sundry supplies," "environmental handling," etc.

Don't be afraid to ask what these mean because this fee is simply a 5 or 10 percent charge tacked onto the total bill. If you object to it, which you certainly should, dealers will often waive it.

You will find that prices for maintenance such as oil changes, alignments, tire rotation and balancing, etc., are usually priced competitively. Where you have to be careful is in the pricing of major repair items, such as transmissions, engines, and air-conditioners.

When quoted a price on a big repair, don't hesitate to negotiate. If you let it be known that you are willing to take your car elsewhere (even if you're bluffing), you can often negotiate the price down significantly.

You should always make an appointment before bringing your car in and it should be scheduled at relatively slow times and days. Avoid bringing your car in early on a Monday morning and other very busy periods.

You want the service adviser to spend as much time with you as is necessary. This will allow you to drive the car with the service adviser if necessary to identify a specific problem such as a squeak, rattle or vibration.

Pick up your car when the service adviser or technician has the time to road test the car with you again to be sure the problem was fixed.

Don't be shy about asking for a loaner car when you have to take your car back a second or third time for a repair that was not done properly. It's the dealership's fault and you should not be inconvenienced.

On a comeback, always talk with the service manager directly. Also always ask that the dealership assign its best technician to the job.

As I have said in earlier chapters, there is nothing more important than choosing the right dealership to do business with. No service department is perfect and never makes a mistake. What you want to find is that service department that, in addition to being competent, will 'fess up to its occasional mistakes, sincerely apologize and make them right.

Section Seven

CONCLUSION

The Future of the Car-Buying Business

Sam Walton reinvented the retail business for just about every product except automobiles. Walmart is now global—the world's largest retailer as well as one of its most profitable and valuable public companies—and has been both praised and vilified.

Detractors include the small businesses and/or inefficient companies it drove out of the market, as well as those who decry its business, employee and environmental practices.

Nevertheless, consumers are drawn in by a combination of its still relatively low prices, numerous outlets and wide selection of products, including groceries in its marketplace stores, and even gas stations in some locations—which add up to convenient, one-stop shopping for busy people.

Let me stop and say right now that I am in no way endorsing Walmart one way or another, nor am I holding it up as an example of what a business should be. My point here is just to show that the business model Sam created changed the way retailing is done and, in the process, simplified and improved the buying experience.

He was able to accomplish what he did by building a retail machine that was more efficient than his competitors. (This efficiency proved a boon in the aftermath of Hurricane Katrina in 2005, when the company was able to marshal its resources to provide relief to residents in the disaster areas faster than lagging government agencies.)

Sam mastered the science and art of purchasing merchandise in volume—first domestically and then later abroad—and tight inventory control, which enabled him to charge some of the lowest prices around.

I have absolutely no doubt that if Sam had been able to sell cars too, he would have figured out a way to do it efficiently with lower pricing. The reason the company sells everything except cars, though, is that state franchise laws protect car dealers from competition like Walmart.

In all 50 states, dealers have been able to lobby their legislators over the years to pass state laws that give them an exclusive market territory.

In Florida, for example, manufacturers may not add another dealer of the same make within a nine-mile radius of the existing dealer. If they attempt to do this, the dealer can appeal to the state department of motor vehicles, where a hearing judge makes the decision.

These franchise laws also tell manufacturers who can retail cars and prohibits manufacturers from owning dealerships, even though a car retailer must have a factory franchise agreement.

The result of all these archaic laws is to put a real damper on competition in the retail car business. It allows inefficient car dealers to remain in business and allows the haggling, horse-trading system of purchasing cars that dates back to the 19th century to perpetuate.

Polls of consumers regularly rank their car-buying and servicing experiences as among the worst for any product or service. Car dealers are consistently ranked among the three professions Americans distrust the most—along with lawyers and politicians.

If we've learned anything from the explosive growth of Walmart, it is that most consumers want low prices and a straightforward buying experience.

Walmart doesn't offer store coupons and doesn't have sales per se, although it does offer clearance items. The price you see is what you get.

Even with today's ever-changing marketplace and modern technology, customers still want a simple, no-haggle buying experience, whether in-store or online. And they want it to be fair.

A consumer doesn't want to go into a retail store, buy a product and find out the next day that her next-door neighbor bought the same item for much less from the same place. This could amount to a difference of hundreds or thousands of dollars when someone buys a car.

Yet this is standard everyday operating procedure for car dealers. Shrewd, educated, sophisticated negotiators can usually buy a car at very close to dealer cost. But the very young, very old, uneducated, naive and/ or those unschooled in speaking English are likely to pay a lot more for the exact same car from that exact same dealer.

I have a hunch, though, that Neanderthal car dealers are nearing extinction. The American consumer is getting smarter and more sophisticated every day. This new, enlightened consumer won't put up much longer with the old way of buying cars.

Customers would scream bloody murder if they walked into Macy's and asked the salesperson for the price of a Samsung big screen TV and the salesman responded, "How much are you willing to pay?" or "I can't give you a price unless you're willing to buy today."

But this is exactly the same thing that happens all the time in most car dealerships today.

The American consumer is also the American voter, however, and I have a feeling that we are about to see some new, pro-consumer legislation with respect as to how cars are sold in America. State franchise laws that help to preserve the status quo will be examined closely.

An example of these kinds of laws and how they work surfaced not so long ago when a start-up company, TrueCar.com, offered a new and refreshing way for car buyers to actually find out what the lowest price in their market was. This lasted about a year and TrueCar.com was growing like wildfire.

I wrote two columns for my local paper about TrueCar.com. You can read them both on my blog, www.earlstewartoncars.com. The first was "Will TrueCar.com Change the Way You Buy a Car In the 21st Century?"

I wrote this before the intense pressure from car dealers, manufacturers and state legislators forced TrueCar.com to accede and redesign its unique, consumer-friendly, lowest-price system.

My later article was called "Online Car-Buying Service TrueCar.com Caves to Pressure by Auto Industry."

Somewhere out there is another Sam Walton-like entrepreneur biding his or her time and waiting for the tolerance level of the American car buyer to flatline when it comes to the way consumers must buy a car today.

I think the founder of TrueCar.com, Scott Painter, could have been that game-changer for the auto-buying industry, but because of the extreme pressure, he gave in.

The American car buyer is waiting for you, Sam or Samantha, and when you are ready, the car-buying world will beat a path to your door.

GLOSSARY OF TERMS

Acquisition fee – fee charged by lender in the lease contract, often marked up by dealer for additional profit

ACV – "actual cash value" – the assessed wholesale value of the trade-in vehicle and the true cost of a used car in the dealer's inventory

Addendum – a decal placed near the Monroney label on a dealer's vehicle that itemizes legitimate and illegitimate add-ons

ADM – "additional dealer mark-up;" artificial and illegitimate inflation of the MSRP of a new vehicle. Similar to a "market adjustment"

ALG – *Automotive Leasing Guide*, a source for vehicle residuals used by leasing companies and industry professionals to gauge things like brand value

ASE – American Service Excellence, national service recognition and accreditation organization

Balloon – a large, lump-sum payment due at the end of certain retail or lease contracts

Best and Worst List – *Consumer Report's* list of recommended and non-recommended vehicles

Black Book – one of several reference guides for used car values. This source is becoming less relevant in the Internet age

Box – dealers' informal term for the finance and insurance (F&I) office: "The Box"

Broker – third party who negotiates a vehicle sale between a buyer and a dealer

Bumper-to-bumper warranty – refers to the manufacturer's comprehensive warranty that covers components other than the engine and transmission. It does not technically cover the bumpers, and it tends to have a much shorter coverage period than the power train warranty.

Buyer's order – the bill of sale that itemizes the price of the vehicle and other charges and fees

Capitalized cost – the "price" of the car on a lease contract. It is basically the "selling price." It can and should be negotiated.

CarFax report – a brand of vehicle history reports that checks for potential problems, such as accidents, odometer rollback, etc.

CSI – Customer Satisfaction Index. the survey-based score that manufacturers use to gauge how well dealers treat their customers. In most cases, this score is meaningless due to manipulation by dealers.

DAP – Delivery Allowance Payment. This is another holdback paid to the dealer by the manufacturer.

Dealer fee – an arbitrary fee added to the price of the vehicle for additional profit to the dealer. Often disguised to appear to be a legitimate local or state fee.

De-horse – a technique used by dealers to prevent customers from shopping further by loaning the vehicle of interest overnight and keeping the trade-in at the dealership. The "horse" is the customer's trade-in.

Depreciation – the reduction in value of a vehicle over time

Disposition fee – fee charged by lenders to the customer at the end of a lease

DMV – Department of Motor Vehicles

Doc stamps – a state fee imposed on retail installment contracts. In Florida it is .35% of the amount financed.

Documentary fee – another term for dealer fee. Same as "doc fee"

Environmental impact fee – a fee added by dealers and independent repair facilities to service invoices. This fee represents additional profit to the dealer. See "shop fee."

Extended service contract/extended warranty – an insurance product sold by dealers and some independent agencies against mechanical breakdown and repair

F&I – Finance & Insurance. This is the step in the car-buying process where final paperwork is completed. It is a profit center where insurance and other products are sold.

FICO – Fair Isaac Corporation

Frame damage/unibody damage – damage to the foundational structure of a vehicle that severely reduces its value and mechanical integrity

GAP – Guaranteed Asset Protection. Insurance sold by the dealer to protect against financial damage resulting from total loss of a vehicle due to damage or theft.

GM – General Manager. Dealership employee in charge of all day-to-day operations. The "boss," second in command to only the owner.

Goodwill repair – Goodwill is what they call all repairs made at no charge when the car is out of warranty.

Holdback – monies returned to the dealer by the manufacturer on every car sold. Holdback is used to inflate the amount of the dealer's vehicle invoice.

Incentives – monies and other offers used to compel a customer to purchase or lease a vehicle. The term generally is used to describe offers made by the manufacturers to the consumer or dealer. See "rebate."

Independent service facility – a non-dealer-affiliated repair facility

Invoice – the "bill of sale" from the manufacturer to the dealer, inflated with holdback

KBB – *Kelley Blue Book.* Consumer-oriented reference guide of used-vehicle values

Labor rate – the hourly rate charged by a dealer for repair and maintenance work

Lease – a contract for use of a vehicle in which the lender purchases the vehicle and charges the customer for depreciation and rent

Lease flip – also known as a "lease conversion," it's the act of switching customers' intended method of payment from a purchase to a lease by convincing them of the supposed advantages of leasing, such as lower monthly payments

Lemon Law – a state law that provides a remedy for consumers who purchase cars that repeatedly fail standards of reliability and performance

List price – the retail asking price for a vehicle – often inaccurately confused with the manufacturer's suggested retail price (see MSRP). This price can be an arbitrary number assigned by the dealer.

Make – manufacturer's brand name

Manufacturer's warranty – an assurance that provides that the vehicle manufacturer assumes the cost of remedying certain defects in parts and workmanship

Market adjustment – an arbitrary inflation of the MSRP of the vehicle by the dealer to take advantage to a real or imagined shortage of supply

Market share – the percentage of sales any particular manufacturer holds in a vehicle sales market – this can be defined locally, regionally, nationally, or globally.

MMR – Manheim Market Reports. An aggregate of vehicle transactions on the wholesale market. Most accurate guide of used vehicle values.

Money factor – the arithmetical construct used to determine the rent charge on a lease. Analogous to the interest rate in an installment contract

Monroney label – the window sticker that must be affixed to all new vehicles for sale until removed by the customer after purchase. This is mandated by federal law and includes such information as the MSRP, EPA rating, etc.

MSRP – Manufacturer's Suggested Retail Price. Not to be confused with "list price," although sometime erroneously used interchangeably.

NADA – National Automobile Dealers Association

OEM – Original Equipment Manufacturer

Out-the-door price – the bottom-line dollar figure you ultimately pay for a vehicle – this will include all fees (legitimate and otherwise) and taxes.

Over-allowance – an inflated trade value presented by the dealer to distract from the selling price of the vehicle. It is effectively a discount (often from an inflated "dealer's list" price).

PDI – Pre-Delivery Inspection, the process of prepping a new vehicle for sale. The cost of this is typically reimbursed to the dealer by the manufacturer.

Power train warranty – component of the manufacturer's warranty that covers the engine, transmission, and transaxle

Puppy-Dogged – technique used by dealers to manipulate customers in becoming emotionally connected to the vehicle of interest by allowing them to keep the vehicle overnight

Quick Quote – an online price quote provided by the dealer

Rebate – money given by the manufacturer to the customer (or dealer) as an incentive for the purchase or lease of a vehicle

Recall – an official order from a manufacturer to address necessary repairs on multiple vehicles

Resale value – the value of a vehicle after a period of ownership

Rescission/bailment agreement – clause affixed to a retail sale that permits the dealer to reclaim possession of a vehicle in the event financing is unobtainable (see Spot delivery)

Residual – the projected value of a vehicle after a certain period of ownership

Sales manager – the dealership personnel responsible for negotiating the sales price of vehicles for the dealer

Service advisor – the dealership personnel responsible for selling service procedures to customers in the service department. Often called "assistant service managers" or "ASMs." These personnel are salespeople.

Service manager – dealership personnel responsible for the day-to-day operations of the service department. The first person to see to resolve an issue in the service department. Do not confuse with ASM or service advisor.

Shop fee – a fee added by dealers and independent repair facilities to service invoices. This fee represents additional profit to the dealer. See "environmental impact fee."

Special finance – term that refers to the sub-prime market for auto loans

Spot delivery – the contracting of a vehicle sale and loan prior to approval from the lender

Stair-step incentives – volume-based cash incentives paid to the dealer by the manufacturer that create uneven vehicle pricing in a market

Stealing the trade/under-allowance – the act of offering a value for a trade to a customer below the appraised value (ACV)

Stock number – an internal reference number used by the dealer to track inventory

TILA – Truth in Lending Act

TSB – Technical Service Bulletin. Not quite a recall, it's guidance provided by the manufacturer to the dealer for remedying known vehicle service issues

VIN – Vehicle Identification Number, also known as "serial number"

Wear and tear – minor damage and degradation caused by normal use of a vehicle over time

Yo-yo – the act of bringing a customer back to re-contract on a vehicle sale because the terms of the loan have been changed. (see Spot delivery)

About the Author

Earl Stewart is the owner of Earl Stewart Toyota in North Palm Beach, Florida, and a consumer advocate who shares his knowledge about the car industry through a weekly newspaper column and radio show.

A native Floridian, Earl was a reluctant car dealer and initially avoided joining his father in the Pontiac dealership the family opened in 1937. After earning a Bachelor of Science degree from the University of Florida and a master's degree in industrial administration from Purdue University, Earl worked as an electronics engineer for four years for Westinghouse Corp.

He joined his father and older brother in the car business in 1968 and helped establish the first Mazda dealership in the eastern United States in 1970. In 1975, the Stewarts secured their Toyota franchise and the dealership, now known as Earl Stewart Toyota, has become one of the most successful Toyota stores in the nation.

Earl has been featured in *The Wall Street Journal, The New York Times, U.S. News & World Report, Businessweek* and other publications. He has made numerous appearances on CNN, Fox News and other news programs.

He is frequently called upon by local and national media to comment on trends in the industry, as well as on his innovative and unorthodox approach to operating an automotive dealership.

All money from the sales of this book will go to charity. Visit http://www.earlstewarttoyota.com/ to see the list of charities and purchase additional copies of this book.